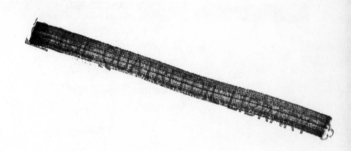

The Q Guide to

Gay Beaches

The Q Guides

FROM ALYSON BOOKS

TRAVEL & LEISURE

Q

GUIDE

OUT THERE

The Q Guide to

Gay Beaches

Stuff You Didn't Know You Wanted to Know . . . about the world's hottest destinations for tans, sand, and sun

[**David Allyn**]

alyson books
NEW YORK

To you, the reader,
for all those hours you've put in at the gym,
all those carbs you've said no to,
and all that money you've spent over the years,
trying to find the perfect swimsuit.
Here's your chance to make it all worthwhile.

© 2008 BY DAVID ALLYN
ALL RIGHTS RESERVED
ALL PHOTOS COURTESY OF THE AUTHOR
MANUFACTURED IN THE UNITED STATES OF AMERICA

THIS TRADE PAPERBACK ORIGINAL IS PUBLISHED BY
ALYSON BOOKS
245 WEST 17TH STREET,
NEW YORK, NY 10011

DISTRIBUTION IN THE UNITED KINGDOM BY
TURNAROUND PUBLISHER SERVICES LTD.
UNIT 3, OLYMPIA TRADING ESTATE,
COBURG ROAD, WOOD GREEN
LONDON N22 6TZ ENGLAND

FIRST EDITION: JANUARY 2008

08 09 10 11 12 13 14 15 16 17 **a** 10 9 8 7 6 5 4 3 2 1

ISBN: 1-59350-041-6
ISBN-13: 978-1-59350-041-2

LIBRARY OF CONGRESS CATALOGING-IN-PUBLICATION DATA
ARE ON FILE.

COVER DESIGN BY VICTOR MINGOVITS

Contents

The author on Ibiza.

Where the Boys Are

QUOTE

"A beach resort is both real and unreal—a collection of houses, streets, bars, dance places: a collection of memories, hopes, illusions, discoveries, distress we experience there at different summers of our lives."

—Andrew Holleran

BEACH TOWNS have a natural attraction for gay men and women. While we may be some of the most creative and productive people on the planet, we have never fully bought into the Protestant work ethic, with its emphasis on perpetually delayed gratification, or Calvinist self-restraint, with its deep-seated sense of propriety. We are inclined to live in the moment, and we prefer our pleasures in pure form. Maybe it's our Greco-Roman heritage or the fact that the sea has always represented escape from the confining forces of civilization, but there's something about the pace and sensuality of beach-town life that perfectly complements gayness the way a piece of pineapple complements a piña colada.

Some may say that the Golden Age of the Gay Beach was the 1970s, post-Stonewall and pre-AIDS, when the major destinations were just being established. But now, with hindsight and a renewed sense of vitality, we're rediscovering those seaside retreats that captivated a previous generation.

At sixteen, I went with my family on vacation to Puerto Rico. One day I wandered off and headed down the shore. Something pulled me down that beach. Soon enough I sensed a change up ahead: a disproportionate number of male sunbathers. And I didn't need any introduction or explanation. I knew immediately that I'd found what I hadn't even been looking for. My discovery gave a whole new flavor to what would otherwise have been an ordinary family vacation, and I began a life-long love affair with gay beaches.

The gay beach holds a special place in the homosexual atlas. P'town, Fire Island, Key West—these are iconographic destinations as critical to our sense of history and cultural cohesion as the Castro, Chelsea, and WeHo. Gay beaches offer the closest thing we have to paradise— both in its most innocent and most decadent connotations. What's more appealing than the sight of a gorgeous guy wearing flip-flops, helplessly licking an ice cream cone as it melts in the sun?

Like many gay men, I am something of a workaholic. I take great pride in my professional accomplishments.

That's another reason many of us are so attracted to beach resorts. There is nothing quite like a reclining beach chair, a frivolous gay novel, and a frozen strawberry daiquiri to calm the mind.

There's a social rhythm to gay beach towns. Unlike straight resorts, which generally cater to couples or families, gay beach towns are shaped by the fact that gay men and women typically move *en masse* in an almost natural flow from breakfast to beach to cocktails to dinner to dancing. That natural rhythm—almost primitive in its simplicity—makes a vacation to a gay beach especially easy for solo travelers. It's impossible not to get swept up in the social tide. With everyone heading in the same direction at the same time, you're bound to meet someone to talk to.

Beach towns are more similar to each other than they are different, but that doesn't negate their individual identities. A day in Provincetown will have a very distinct feel compared to one in South Beach. Regional differences, though subtle and rapidly disappearing, are worth seeking out. Step off the gay beater path. Get your coffee at a bodega in Key West. Eat salt water taffy in Rehoboth. The better you get to know a place, the longer you will remember your vacation afterwards.

This book is meant to serve the needs of three different audiences: those who have never set foot on a gay beach, those who have been to a few gay beaches but are looking for a new one to explore, and those who are weary of rehashed truisms and seek new insight into familiar places. Whichever category you find yourself in, my hope is that your interest in gay beach life is piqued and your senses aroused. Life is short, so you might as well strip down, spread on the suntan lotion, and smile at that guy a few towels away on the sand.

It is easy to treat a gay beach trip as an occasion merely for drunken revelry. After all, what's better than an afternoon tea dance with disco classics and friends in high spirits? But while the Dionysian aspect of gay beaches is an essential part of their appeal, I hope you will seek out more nuanced, "Apollonian" experiences as well. Go for an early morning jog or stay up late merely to read a good book while listening to the crashing of the waves. If the vastness of the ocean can teach us anything, it is that our most frenzied, orgiastic activities are brief eddies of entertainment compared to the ancient and eternal currents of the universe. I have come to believe that a proper beach vacation consists of four parts merriment, two parts mirth, and one part pure melancholy.

Beaches, especially gay beaches, have a communitarian spirit. My various visits to gay beaches over the years have aroused deep feelings of connectedness, of belonging, of being part of a much larger whole. But they have also, at times, triggered equally profound feelings of loneliness and anomie. That, I believe, is the contradictory nature and power of gay resorts. On the one hand, congregating by the sea can liberate us from our daily routines and identities, allowing us to meld into a common humanity (at least, a common gay humanity). But the vastness of the sea—as well as the often cruelly judgmental nature of gay culture—can underscore our essential aloneness. The choice is to resist the dichotomous nature of the beach or embrace it, and I highly recommend the latter. Laugh, cry, skinny-dip; do something you would never do at home. At the beach, it's worth being as gay as you can possibly be.

Traveling Abroad

Like most travel writers, I am of the firm belief that it is important to see the world. Spending time in a foreign country—eating new foods, learning new customs, getting miserably lost, and falling in love with men who don't speak English—is essential to living the well-lived life. And if you're going to travel abroad, there's no reason not to include a gay beach or two on your itinerary.

"Next year in Mykonos" ought to be the gay equivalent of the Jewish expression, "Next year in Jerusalem." After thousands of years of conquest, development, and tourist invasion, Mykonos remains next to perfect.

Ibiza has become the world's party capital. That means loud music, lots of alcohol, and plenty of drugs. If this is your scene, go for it. If you're passing through on a cruise, make sure you take a moment to appreciate the Old Town's stunning grandeur.

Q FACT

Many hotels and guesthouses in popular areas have a three- or four-night minimum stay. Even so, the better ones tend to fill up fast. A gay beach vacation requires some careful planning well in advance of your travel.

LOSING YOUR GAY BEACH VIRGINITY

Are you a gay beach virgin? Then congratulations on considering your first foray onto a gay beach: hallowed homosexual ground. I believe that at some point in every gay man's life, the time comes to don a Speedo and hit a gay beach. It's a little like coming out all over again, only this time you're coming out to a gazing public of fellow queers waiting to check you out. Depending on your level of self-confidence, it can range from thrilling to intimidating. Still, it's a rite of passage that really can't be avoided if one is going to live a fully fledged gay life.

Below are a few tips for your "first time." Bear in mind, every gay beach is different, with its own customs and rules, but here are few generalizations that should help you get acclimated quickly:

1. Bring something to lie on. Gay beaches are rarely equipped with umbrellas and other accoutrements

Sitges is Ibiza's great uncle: wiser, calmer, and more refined. Situated just thirty minutes from Barcelona, Sitges is the gay beach capital of Spain. Go for the day or for three days—either way, you'll be glad you did.

that you might find at more upscale, hetero resorts. With a few notable exceptions, gay beaches are strictly BYOB: Bring Your Own Blanket.

2. Be prepared for a hike. Gay beaches are often out of the way and can be downright difficult to get to. The beach in Provincetown, for instance, is a good half-mile hike through wet marshes. Don't bring more than you really need on your first day. Leave the boom box at home.

3. If you're going with a group, pay attention to how you get to and from your lodgings. Who knows? You may not choose to go home with the same people you arrived with.

4. Gay beaches usually have a cruising area, most often near the dunes, away from the water. If you sit near the dunes, expect to be cruised.

5. Smile. Nothing is as attractive as a bright smile on a guy's face. In new situations, it's always tempting to try to be invisible or act cool, but that can come off as arrogant. A friendly smile will attract attention and invite conversation.

The straights have Cancún, but we have Puerto Vallarta, and given the town's charm, we got the better end of the deal.

The Q Guide to
Gay Beaches

You never know who you'll meet at the beach.

CHAPTER ONE

The History of Gay Sunbathing (The Abridged, Beach-Read Version)

THE HISTORY of the gay beach really begins in the 1920s, when the world's fabulous found the French Riviera. Influential artists like openly gay Cole Porter and Jean Cocteau turned St. Tropez and the rest of the South of France into a fashion-lover's paradise.

Not to be outdone, New York's Broadway types, bohemian artists, and prominent writers (read: "gay people") established their own private enclave on Fire Island, a thin stretch of land running parallel to Long Island. They built makeshift cottages and established a tiny town called the Grove. While it was all destroyed in a 1938 hurricane, the gays were undeterred. They rebuilt their homes and turned the Grove into *the* place to be. Truman Capote, W. H. Auden, Christopher Isherwood,

Q FACT

In 1964, when most young men were still wearing ties and jackets on campus, a young rebel named Jefferson Poland staged a nude "wade-in" off the coast of San Francisco to protest social attitudes toward sexuality. Describing himself as bisexual, Poland went on to found the Sexual Freedom League and organized the nation's first protest against military policies toward homosexuals.

and James Baldwin were just some of the famous gay literary types to summer in the Grove.

By the fifties, Fire Island was just one of several shore-lines in the country where gays and lesbians were heading to seek each other out. The war had shaken things up—boys came back men—and, with the spread of cars and jobs, it was relatively easy for a single person to move to a new town and start a new life. Still, this was the era of police raids and domestic anxiety, so discretion was of the utmost importance. The trick, then, was to find places the cops would ignore or overlook—and remote beaches were the perfect answer.

The most popular gay sites of the fifties, apart from the towns of Fire Island, were Key West, Provincetown, and the "North Beach" of San Francisco. Like Fire Island, they attracted their share of bohemians and rebels, who were either gay or openly experimental. At the top of the cultural food chain, Key West and Provincetown shared Tennessee Williams; North Beach had the Beats—Jack Kerouac, Allen Ginsberg, and their various writing and sexual partners.

Meanwhile, back in Europe, the French Riviera continued to attract intellectual and fashionable gays. Simone de Beauvoir, Rudolph Nureyev, Tab Hunter, and Rudi Gernreich, among countless others, chose to summer and seduce in the South of France.

In the 1970s, gay life came into its own. The rise of jet travel, the worldwide relaxation of social mores, and, of course, Stonewall, fostered an era of personal freedom. Just as gay men from around the globe flocked to San Francisco and New York, they built a new capital of global decadence on Mykonos, a blue and white paradise in the middle of the Aegean, ruled over by the spirit of Dionysus. The "Three D's" of the 1970s—drugs, disco, and debauchery—put Mykonos on the map as the ultimate gay resort.

Back to the Beginning

Which takes us back to Ancient Greece, when sun worship was a part of daily life. In fact, it's nice to remember, as you're lying on the sand, soaking up the rays—thinking about nothing more pressing than your next sip of alcohol, your next romantic liaison—that you are participating in an ancient and honored custom older than the majority of our most revered institutions. The Greeks called it "heliotherapy," from *helio* for "sun" and *therapy* for "time spent lying prostrate thinking about nothing but yourself" (the Greeks, in their infinite wisdom, invented a kind of therapy that doesn't even require health insurance).

The Greeks must have appreciated the link between sun worship and gayness, because they envisioned their god of the sun, Helios, as a young stud with a fancy crown and a shiny chariot. Helios was often depicted with his favorite animal, the cock. On the island of Rhodes, where guys really got into the whole Helios thing, they would do naked gymnastics in his honor. (In the classical era, as Helios evolved into the god we know as Apollo, he became increasingly associated with the power of male beauty. Legend developed that the gorgeous and very gay Apollo and his dykey sister Artemis were born as orphans on the sun-kissed island of Delos, just off the coast of Mykonos.)

Lena Lenček and Gideon Bosker, authors of *The Beach: The History of Paradise on Earth*, write: "In classical myth, the shoreline is typically a place where identity itself is imperiled and the self becomes unrecognizable—sometimes diminished, sometimes augmented, according to the whimsy of the gods." Remember that as you're making eyes with the god on the blanket next to yours.

Throughout the ancient world, it seems, sun worship was often linked, at least loosely, to homosexuality. In ancient Japan, the myth of the sun goddess had a lesbian element. One day, the sun goddess Amaterasu got upset and decided to hide in a cave. (You know how tempermental sun goddesses can be.) This had the unfortunate effect of making the whole world dark. It was only when another goddess, the goddess of the dawn, did an erotic dance that Amaterasu came out. The myth implies a romantic, even sexual, bond between the two goddesses. Amaterasu couldn't be cheered up by anyone but the lithe and dainty dawn. In ancient Egypt, where sun worship was even more popular than it was in Greece, priests encouraged the veneration of the sun god, Ra. Mankind was said to be born from Ra's sweat. Now that's a homoerotic idea if I've ever heard one. (Of course, we shouldn't be surprised that it was probably the gays who were behind all that ancient myth-making anyway. Who else could have come up with such flamboyant characters and deliciously high drama?)

Our own conflicted attitudes toward sunbathing can be traced back to the Romans. Like the Greeks, the Romans were a coastal people. In fact, well-to-do Romans established beach resorts throughout the Mediterranean. Baiae was the principal beach resort of the Roman world for five hundred years. It was considered the ultimate party town, with abundant opportunities for both hetero and homo activity. The story goes that the waters of Baiae were too cold to swim in—until handsome young Eros took a dip and heated them up. Ever after, anyone who swam in Baiae was destined for amour.

Roman men, like their Greek forebears, probably did most of their swimming in the nude, but surviving murals from Pompeii suggest that Roman women wore two-piece suits that foreshadowed the modern bikini.

The Romans often wanted shelter from the hot sun as much as they wanted opportunities to tan. Hence, they built cool, indoor bathhouses to escape the heat. (We all know what ended up going on in those bathhouses.) And—eager to distinguish themselves from their darker-skinned Jewish, Arab, and African slaves—Roman women would paint their faces white to avoid looking tan. (The practice was unwise, as ancient paints often contained toxic lead.) In other words, the Romans were ambivalent about the sun, and they passed down their ambivalence to succeeding generations.

The Early Christians did all they could to stamp out sunbathing, viewing it as decadent and pagan. Needless to say, they disapproved of all Greek and Roman customs involving social nudity and homosexuality. By the end of antiquity and the beginning of the Dark Ages, therefore, sun worship was all but taboo. Clothes got heavier and heavier until you ended up with the thick vestments of monks and Crusaders.

(One group of early Christians stands out for its endorsement of sunbathing. The Adamites believed the whole point of religion was to reestablish Adam and Eve's state of original innocence. Calling their church "Paradise," they practiced nude sunbathing, rejected marriage, and embraced sensuality. Sadly but not surprisingly, they were persecuted and eradicated by their more "moral" brothers and sisters.)

Organized sunbathing—or any sunbathing—was probably unheard of during the Middle Ages. Medieval Europeans feared both water and bathing—believing that bathing led to disease. (Hence the spread of diseases like the plague in the fourteenth century.) They actually thought bathing could lead to the penetration of the skin by disease-bearing agents.

In the Americas, Africa, and Polynesia, forms of public nudity were common, of course. But Christian missionaries, wherever they went, tried their best to foster a sense of shame.

Cultural elitism and Christian notions of chastity combined to make suntanning disreputable. In the European mind, "pale," "wan," and "fair" grew synonymous with virginal, which was equal to virtuous. It's ridiculously silly that medieval depictions of Jesus and Mary portrayed them as fair-skinned (sometimes even fair-haired) Northern Europeans who looked like they'd never spent a day outdoors—despite the fact that they'd been Jews who'd lived in the scorching heat of the desert.

Shakespeare captured early modern anxieties about skin color and the cultural importance of paleness in *Much Ado About Nothing*, in which Beatrice (Act II, Scene I), feeling sorry for herself and her dim marital prospects, complains: "Thus goes every one to the world but I, and I am sunburnt; I may sit in a corner and cry heigh-ho for a husband!"

As in Ancient Rome, the cultural preference for fair skin that held sway in early modern Europe was rooted in social class distinctions. To have fair, unfreckled skin meant that one was above outdoor, manual labor. Peasants and farmers were tan from long hours of outdoor work. Whiteness was associated with wealth. Brown skin meant poverty, vulgarity, and lack of social status. It was perilously close to the "black" skin of the Africans and the "red" skin of the Native Americans. On the European continent, eighteenth-century royals and aristocrats took pains to powder their faces in clouds of white, in order to make themselves look as wan as possible. They also began carrying parasols and even wearing masks to protect themselves from the sun. Eighteenth-century women who wished to go for an outdoor dip wore specially designed bathing gowns, heavy fabric with weights sewed into the hems to prevent the fabric from floating upwards.

Q FACT

In the nineteenth century, the urge to travel by sea was considered a sign of mental illness and homosexuality.

Sun worship, once glorified by the Greeks, had, by the early modern era, become seriously despised. But the industrialization of Europe was about to change that. The more densely populated that cities become, the more people tend to seek flight to the seashore.

Victorian Vices

The West witnessed a brief moment of rationalism in the late 1700s and early 1800s, as science and philosophy outpaced religion. Benjamin Franklin advocated the naked "air bath." Thoreau would take naked walks. Even President John Quincy Adams is said to have swum nude in the Potomac.

But as the Victorian era reached its height, so did a new-found obsession with sexual and moral purity. The Victorians, of course, insisted on covering every inch of skin. But the more the Victorians layered their clothes, the more they wanted to take them off—preferably at the beach.

Seaside, the Victorians were befuddled. They yearned to enjoy the frivolities of public bathing, but they felt pressured to maintain their modesty. So they donned elaborate bathing costumes that today one could wear to work in a Chicago winter. Victorian anxieties persisted into the twentieth century. In 1907, the Australian swimmer Annette Kellerman—the first woman to attempt to swim the English Channel—was arrested on a Massachusetts beach for wearing a one-piece swimsuit that showed off her arms and legs.

(All of this Victorian focus on female modesty had its advantages for men inclined toward same-sex sensuality. For, if mixed bathing required heavy attire, boys alone could still have their fun. No one thought twice of boys swimming naked together as long as there were no girls around. In fact, many encouraged naked, single-sex swimming for men as a healthy and invigorating diversion from the effeminizing effects of the industrial age. Hence the birth of the Young Men's Christian Association, with its nude-only swimming policies.)

Eventually, the bohemians of the 1910s and the flappers of the 1920s would rebel against their parents' and grandparents' prudery. Everything from dresses to swimwear grew more revealing. Meanwhile, the growth of the middle class and the movement of young women into the paid labor force in the early decades of the twentieth century led to the advent of "leisure time" and spawned a new industry of amusement parks, boardwalks, and seaside resorts.

The First Tan Lines

Legend has it that the craze for bronzed skin began in 1923 when famous fashion designer Coco Chanel accidentally acquired a deep tan during a vacation on the French Riviera. With or without Chanel, the beach was destined to be rediscovered in the twentieth century. "There was no one at Antibes this summer," F. Scott Fitzgerald wrote of the French resort, "except me,

Zelda, the Valentinos, the Murphys, Mistinguiett, Rex Ingram, Dos Passos, Alice Terry, the MacLeishes, Charles Brackett, Maude Kahn, Esther Murphy, Marguerite Namara, E. Phillips Oppenheim, Mannes the violinist, Floyd Dell, May and Chrystal Eastman, ex-Premier Orlando, Etienne de Beaumont." Beaches had become the place to escape the city.

During World War II, pinups of bathing beauties were all the rage. Sunbathing was further helped along in the 1940s by the introduction of the "bikini," named after the famous Bikini Atoll nuclear weapons test (in those days, nuclear weapons tests were seen as happily reassuring of Western military dominance). The bikini's inventors said they chose the name because they believed the two-piece suit was likely to cause as much a commotion as the nuclear explosion itself.

During World War II, sailors stationed overseas would often sunbathe on the decks of their ships. Photographs of the era convey a playfully homoerotic ambience.

But it was in the 1960s, on the heels of the postwar baby boom, that beach culture really took off. Brian Hyland's 1960 pop song "Itsy Bitsy Teenie Weenie Yellow Polka Dot Bikini" foreshadowed a new era of revelry. And a series of Hollywood films (the first ones starring Annette Funicello and Frankie Avalon) portrayed the American beach as the quintessential site of adolescent freedom, friendship, and romantic adventure. *Beach Party* (1963), *Muscle Beach Party* (1964), *Bikini Beach* (1964), *Pajama Party* (1964) (with Jesse White and Ben Lessy), *Beach Blanket Bingo* (1965), and *How to Stuff a Wild Bikini* propelled teenagers toward the sand.

TIPS FOR TUCKING IN THE NOT-SO-PERFECT TUMMY

When you're not a muscle bunny, it's tempting to stay away from the beach. But a few tips of the trade can help you win admirers no matter what your shape. The key is playing tricks on the eye.

1. If you're young and you've got just a bit of a paunch, wear a loose-fitting tank top. A loose-fitting tank can help hide the extra flesh and will give you that "half-dressed" look that adds spice. If possible, choose a tank with vertical stripes—they always have a thinning effect.

2. If you've got a true beer belly, embrace it. Go shirtless, but wear long, sheer or blousy pants. First off, lots of guys think a beer belly is hot. Second, long, sheer pants (which can be purchased online from N2N Bodywear, www.n2nbodywear.com) will readily stand out on a beach and make others want to see what you've got underneath.

3. Avoid horizontal stripes at all costs. They only make things worse.

4. Go naked. The men on nude beaches tend to be less toned than those on regular beaches and are generally less judgmental. It's a more hippie-dippy, be-and-let-be attitude. Besides, when others can see "everything," they won't be looking at your navel.

Q FACT

In the 1980s, lesbian feminists launched the "topfree" movement to protest dissimilar decency laws for men and women. Topfree activism led to several arrests and court cases. In 1992, New York's highest state court ruled that the law cannot discriminate. Accordingly, in the state of New York women have the right to be topfree wherever men do.

In the sixties, Americans also became aware of a thriving American subculture—nudism. The first nudist clubs and parks were established in the 1930s, and they continued to attract members through the war and postwar years. In a landmark 1958 Supreme Court case, nudists won the right to send uncensored nudist magazines through the mails. By the sixties, it would have been hard *not* to know about nudism.

The nudist victory over censorship had tremendous implications for gay life in America. Soon enough, magazines aimed at the gay male reader were readily available. That made it possible for gays in one part of the country to find out what gays were doing in other parts of the country. Information about gay beaches spread. Even in the '60s, these spots tended to be hard to get to—close to the major cities, but enough out of the way so as to avoid harassment or unwanted attention. But as more and more men came out in the 1970s, secrecy and seclusion became less important. Gay beach resorts like Key West, Provincetown, and the Pines surged in popularity, making the annual (or, in some cases, weekend) gay beach vacation almost de rigueur for every self-respecting gay man.

The Gay Beach Today

To this day, gay beaches are special places. Gay life may be more accepted than ever before, but gays—particularly gay men—often prefer to vacation together, free to wear the skimpiest of swimsuits without fear of offending any families.

Gay beaches remain more of an East Coast phenomenon than a West Coast one. Perhaps that's because East Coast gays have tended to be more separatist than their West Coast brothers and sisters (and East Coast cities have tended to be less inclusive). Or it may be because, in the first half of the twentieth century, closeted Hollywood celebrities would typically come East to escape the tabloids and gossip reporters. Gay beaches grew up where these celebrities came to play. A final explanation is that West Coast cities like L.A. and San Diego are really overgrown beach towns themselves. Whichever theory you prefer, East Coast beaches remain key "destinations" on the gay cultural map.

Personally, I believe the gay beach is a special spot—not just for showing off one's abs (it will always be that), but for reading the great works of gay fiction, for painting a picture of one's lover in the late afternoon light, for writing novels and plays, for meeting thoughtful and engaging characters, for appreciating the sensuality of nature, for enjoying good food and witty conversation, for remembering the special privilege it is, as writer

Ethan Mordden would say, "to be a citizen of gay." In the everyday world, gays make life beautiful. In the twilight evenings of our beach houses and summer cottages, with the waves crashing in the distance and the salty taste of heartbreak never far away, we remember the beauty of life.

CHAPTER TWO

Partying in Provincetown

"We joke that at 8:45 every night a siren goes off announcing, 'Attention all heterosexuals. Provincetown will be closing in fifteen minutes. Please bring your purchases to the register. Thank you for shopping in P'town. Now get the hell out.'"

—William J. Mann, *The Men from the Boys*

NOTHING ABOUT Provincetown conforms to the traditional rules of society. First, take the narrow strip of Commercial Street. On any day of the week it is jammed with people walking, biking, rollerblading, pushing their infants in strollers. But the street is still a street, and cars force their way through the crowds, creating a chaos unlike anything outside an amusement park. If that weren't enough, drag queens on roller skates slip through the traffic, hawking their evening shows. Then there's the beach, a good mile walk through marshes that flood in the late afternoon. The beach is rocky and uncomfortable and altogether dismal, but still packed with boys.

New Yorkers sometimes forget that people in other parts of the country actually go on vacation to relax. For New Yorkers, the idea of throwing on a pair of old shorts and a T-shirt, having fried clams for lunch, and going for a bike ride can seem like a fantasy out of a Hollywood movie. But in Provincetown, that's exactly how you'll spend your days, and you'll be very happy indeed.

P'town is popular with straights and gays alike (on summer weekends, families pour into town from all over the cape), but it is the queers who have made it famous. Gays make up the majority of property owners, city officials, etc. And even though the Pines and Cherry Grove are more exclusively gay in terms of summer visitors, P'town is an actual town, so the fact that it is "gay-owned and operated" year-round feels striking. Anyone who's been to Fire Island knows that it is an escape from reality; Provincetown is a reality of its own.

Ultimately, what's remarkable about Provincetown is the fact that *gays rule*. At any given moment, the gays may be far outnumbered by the straights, but no one can doubt that the gays are in charge. Most of the property owners are gay, the guesthouses are gay-owned, the stores fly gay flags, the evening shows all feature drag performers. The families who come with their young children for the weekend are visitors, here on our sufferance. Basically, it's a world turned upside down.

Originally a Portuguese fishing village that later became a haven for writers and painters and which quickly earned a queer reputation, Provincetown is what Tennessee Williams dubbed the "frolicsome tip of the cape." Recently, with Massachusetts becoming the first state in the union to grant legal recognition to gay marriages, Provincetown has seen a surge of popularity amongst gay couples.

Provincetown's Major Attractions

1. Sunbathing and Tea at the Boatslip Hotel. It's like being on the lido deck of a 1950s cruise ship. You're lying there by the pool, amidst the glistening bodies, and all of a sudden a voice from the heavens announces the hour. Then, in unison, a hundred beach chairs are turned ninety degrees. Because Provincetown's beach is such a disappointment, the Boatslip, which overlooks Provincetown Bay, is really a better option. Lounge chairs are available for five dollars and a towel for three. Smiling waiters will gladly bring you drinks from the bar, but plan on spending seven dollars for a watered-down daiquiri. At 5 o'clock, the chairs are put away and the music begins for the early evening Tea Dance.

2. The drag shows. You'd have to be a member of Al-Qaeda not to be amused by P'town's drag talent. You'll

know which queens are performing because you'll see them all on Commercial Street, rolling through town on skates, barking the straights and gays alike. Some of the more famous performers include Varla Jean Merman, Windsor Newton, Trinity, and Teeny Tiny Tina Turner. A true classic is "Showgirls" at the Crown and Anchor, an amateur drag contest with a $500 prize.

3. The Atlantic House (better known as the "A-House"). Whether or not you go for the club music, at least stop by to see the men's room of this hotel-turned-disco, with its walls famously covered floor to ceiling in cut-outs from your favorite gay men's magazines. The Atlantic House was originally a rooming house where Tennessee Williams once stayed in the summer of 1940 and had an affair with a young blond.

4. Pizza at Spiritus. P'town is located in Puritan Massachusetts, so it should come as no surprise that evening activities end much earlier than in most other resorts. But as soon as the bars close, everyone convenes on the steps of Spiritus Pizza (190 Commercial Street) for a 1 a.m. snack. By 2 a.m. on any summer night, the street outside Spiritus is packed with upwards of five hundred guys. It's a little like being back in college in the days before coeducation.

5. Renting a bike. First of all, you'll need one just to get to the beach. Second, though it may seem like an extreme sport, what with all the cars and trucks and pedestrian traffic crowded onto Commercial Street, riding a bike through town is worth the risk just to know you've done it. More serious riders will want to bike through the nature preserves just outside town. I

thought this seemed like a good idea till I was frantically peddling uphill to keep pace with my peers and I realized I was no longer on vacation. At which point, I rode back into town, headed for the pier, and comforted myself with an ice cream. There are four rental shops in town with comparable prices. Bikes can be rented for $75–$100 a week at Ptown Bikes (42 Bradford St.).

Sand

The easiest way to get to Herring Cove Beach is . . . oops, I forgot, there is no easy way. No matter how you do it, it's a schlep. The standard route is as follows: First, ride your bike down Bradford Street (about half a mile). When you get to the end, you'll see a cluster of bike racks. Lock up your bike, take all your belongings and prepare for the trek. Now, follow the crowds and walk twenty minutes through the marshes. (Enjoy the moment: these same marshes will likely be flooded on your way back). Take a left when you get to the "beach." Don't bother looking for the smooth sand—you won't find any.

Calories

Dining in Provincetown is hit-or-miss. There are plenty of restaurants in town, but it's easy to pay for a meal that's not worth the price. Service is often subpar, too, perhaps due to the fact that the gratuity is often added directly to the bill. Most of the time you would do best just getting some fried clams or chicken strips at Mojo's on the pier.

Most visitors will want to stop at the Lobster Pot (321 Commercial St.), a veritable factory of a restaurant with 104 employees that has been in operation since 1978. (The food is a gamble: the lobster bisque is very tasty, but the fish and chips not so much) No less harried than any of the other serving staff, my waiter turned out to be one of the owners of the restaurant; his brother was busy as head chef in the kitchen.

Café Heaven (199 Commercial St.) is great for people-watching, but the food leaves something to be desired.

For a hearty breakfast, head to Café Edwidge (333 Commercial St.).

By far the best dinner to be had in Provincetown is at the Red Inn (15 Commercial St.) in the west end of town. Although the inn is over two hundred years old (FDR and Eleanor stayed at the inn on a visit to Provincetown), it was redone about five years ago. The new owners—four gay men—have done an excellent job of turning the restaurant into an itinerary stop of its own. For reservations, call 866-473-3466.

Bar Tab

Most of Provincetown's "bars" are located in the various guesthouses, giving the whole place—even the various leather bars—a fairly tame feel. And true to its Protestant heritage, Provincetown is an early town. If you intend to go out, start early: maybe as early as 4 p.m. at the Boatslip (161 Commercial St.) for Tea Dance.

The Atlantic House, also known as the "A-House" (6 Masonic Pl.) is like a mini gay university, offering everything you could want in a single, campuslike setting. There's dance music, a leather bar, and a bar for older men.

The Crown & Anchor (247 Commercial St.) plays Yale to the Atlantic House's Harvard. Here you can choose between a standard nightclub at the Paramount, or the outdoor Poolside Grill & Raw Bar.

Continuing our Ivy League metaphor, don't miss out on Provincetown's equivalent of Princeton: the Gifford House (11 Carver St.), which has a porch lounge, a piano bar, and a quasi-leather club.

Finally, the Vixen (336 Commercial St.), catering to women, is Provincetown's Wellesley. Located at the Pilgrim House Inn, the Vixen has a wine bar, dance club, and restaurant.

Bedding

P'town has some summer shares (a throwback to its days as an authentic artists' retreat), but these days it's really a guesthouse culture. Many of the guesthouses have five-night minimum stays.

The Admiral's Landing (158 Bradford) is a quaint guesthouse owned by a married gay couple who are experts on all things Provincetown. The muffins are freshly baked, the book and video libraries are well stocked, and the Jacuzzi is open till eleven. Rates: $110–$140; Ph.: 800-934-0925; www.admiralslanding.com.

The Anchor Inn (175 Commercial St.) has its own private beach and a majestic feel. Sixteen rooms have waterfront balconies overlooking the harbor. All guestrooms and common areas are smoke-free, however smoking is permitted on balconies adjoining the room

MORE PROVINCETOWN GUESTHOUSES

Aerie House (184 Bradford, 800-487-1197)

Ampersand (6 Cottage, 800-574-9645)

Beaconlight (12 Winthrop, 800-696-9603)

Benchmark (6 Dyer; 888-487-7440)

Bradford Carver (70 Bradford; 800-826-9083)

Carpe Diem (12 Johnson; 508-487-4242)

Carriage House (7 Central; 800-309-0248)

Christopher's By the Bay (8 Johnson; 877-487-9263)

The Commons (386 Commercial; 800-487-0784)

Crown and Anchor (247 Commercial; 508-487-1430)

Gallery Inn (3 Johnson; 800-676-3010)

Gifford House (11 Carver; 800-434-0130)

John Randall House (140 Bradford; 800-573-6700)

Seasons (160 Bradford; 800-563-0113)

White Wind (174 Commercial; 888-449-9463)

or outdoor areas. Rates: $115–$385; Ph.: 800-858-6257; www.anchorinnbeachhouse.com.

The Brass Key (67 Bradford St.) is actually nine properties surrounding a pool, forming a single compound. Arguably the most luxurious place to stay in Provincetown. Rates: $235–$485; Ph.: 800-842-9858; www.brasskey.com.

PROVINCETOWN'S THEME WEEKS

Provincetown is famous for its theme weeks, so book your vacation accordingly.

Provincetown International Film Festival: mid-June
Circuit Party: Week of 4th of July
Bear Week: mid-July
Family Week: late July
Carnival Parade: mid-August
Women's Week: early October
Transgender Week: mid-October

Provincetown's Saturday Schedule

Provincetown runs on its own "Saturday Schedule." That is to say, visitors arrive on Saturday and leave the following Saturday. There is no point in booking a room through to the final Sunday morning—everyone you met over the week will be gone by Saturday afternoon and a new cast of characters will have arrived. Staying over till Sunday can leave you feeling depressed, both because the party is over, and a new one, that you won't be staying for, is about to begin.

Provincetown's Saturday Schedule is embedded in the town's theme-week system. Bear Week, for instance, will begin on a Saturday and end seven days later. So will Family Week, Women's Week, and Carnival Week.

In and Out

Provincetown is a two-hour drive from Boston (seven hours from New York). A better option is the high-speed, ninety-minute ferry that costs $69 round-trip and leaves Boston three times a day (www.boston -ptown.com). On the weekends, slower, less-expensive ferry service ($20 for a three-hour ride) is available as well. You won't need (or want) a car in town, so it's well worth taking the ferry.

QUOTE

"In my more wistful moments, I think of Provincetown as an academy: an institution of education where students apprentice themselves and learn from willing teachers how to be gay."

—John Preston

Pages

Provincetown attracts writers and readers alike. Michael Thomas Ford's *Last Summer* is a fun novel of love and lust with Ford's trademark style of ensemble storytelling. William J. Mann's poignant novels *The Men from the Boys* and *Where the Boys Are* explore the yearning for love—romantic and platonic—that lies beneath the nonstop partying of the circuit-scene. John Preston's *Franny, the Queen of Provincetown: A Novel* is, despite its subtitle, more a play than a novel. The text consists of a collection of monologues. Nikki Baker's *The Lavender House Murders* has an African-American protagonist. *By the Sea Shore* by Sandra Morris is another lesbian mystery. If you like mysteries (and Provincetown does seem the perfect setting for an old-fashioned tale of middle-of-the-night murder), also check out Jessica Thomas, *Caught in the Net: An Alex Peres Mystery*. Karen Christel Krahulik's *Provincetown: From Pilgrim Landing to Gay Resort* provides a solid history of our favorite town.

The Provincetown Paradox

Why did the Pilgrims flee Mother England? You probably studied this question in elementary school. What you surely did not learn was that one of the reasons the Pilgrims left England was that they did not like the fact that the king, James I, was openly gay. James I had a lover and said, "Jesus Christ did the same, and therefore I cannot be blamed. Christ had his John, and I have my George." This didn't sit well with the Pilgrims, then known as Brownists, and they were very public in their dissent. James I told the Brownists they could accept his

QUESTIONS TO ASK WHEN BOOKING A GUESTHOUSE RESERVATION

1. How far is the house from the center of town? Any answer other than, "we're right in the heart of town," is a red flag. (Don't bother asking how far the house is from the beach because the gay section of the beach may very well be far away from everything).

2. Is the property clothing optional? A yes answer usually indicates a highly sexually charged environment.

3. Is the house mixed or single-sex (again, another indication of how sexually charged the environment is likely to be).

4. Is there off-street parking?

5. Does the house provide bikes, beach towels, umbrellas (for both sun and rain), and/or breakfast? Of course, if you intend to bring Fido, or even if you simply have allergies, remember to ask if pets are allowed.

version of Christianity or leave the country. The Brownists chose the latter, first heading for Amsterdam and then for Massachusetts. They settled at Plymouth, just across the bay from what is now Provincetown. Ironically, the Pilgrims turned out to be some of the most liberal-minded of the new settlers, bequeathing to New England a strain of open-mindedness that has persisted to this day. Were James I to arrive at Provincetown today, he could not only "have his George," he could marry him too.

CHAPTER THREE

Free on Fire Island

QUOTE

"[H]ere we find gay stripped to its essentials. The beautiful are more fully exposed here, the trolls more cast out than anywhere else—thus their pride and passion. The beguiling but often irrelevant data of talent and intelligence that can seem enticing in the city are internal contradictions in a place without an opera house or a library. Only money and charm count. Professional advantages are worthless,

> for, in a bathing suit, all men
> have the same vocation. Yet
> there are distinctions of
> rank. Those who rent are the
> proletariat, those who own
> houses are the bourgeoisie,
> and houseboys form the
> aristocracy."
>
> —Ethan Mordden, *I've a Feeling We're
> Not in Kansas Anymore*

IN THE HISTORY of gay letters, many words have been spilled over Fire Island, a true "fantasy island" for gay men and women, only two and a half hours from New York. A thin wisp of land, bordered on one side by a bay and on the other by the Atlantic Ocean, Fire Island has, for many, become synonymous with gaydom. The island actually has several straight towns, but they are as relevant to the Island's mythology as Coca-Cola is to a Cosmo. The two points of interest on the island for gays are The Pines and Cherry Grove, the former for the boys and the latter primarily for the girls.

For a young gay man who can afford a weekend on the island, the Pines is as close to perfection as one can

Q FACT

The Pines and Cherry Grove are located on Fire Island (about 50 miles east of New York City). Fire Island is a thin strip of an island, approximately 35 miles long and, at its widest points, half a mile across. It runs parallel with Long Island, and the two are separated by the Great South Bay.

get. First you have the beach: one long stretch of golden sand. Probably the best on the entire East Coast. The water is clean, the dunes carefully preserved. You won't find litter here the way you will in Fort Lauderdale or loud music as in Miami. The beach is pristine, welcoming, relaxing. Then there are the houses. The Pines consists of dozens of sprawling bungalows, each with a perfectly appointed kitchen, a giant hot tub, and an outdoor shower. Then there are the pathways: wood-planked runs that lead you through the pine trees to your next adventure. No cars are allowed on the island. And finally there are the people: the gay boys and men who flock from the city every weekend and have turned the Pines into the summer capital of gay life. Forget the Hamptons with its bumper-to-bumper traffic, its Upper East Side pretensions, its overpriced restaurants. In the Pines, it's gay summer camp for adults. You inhale the evergreen air, you stroll casually in your Speedo and flip-flops with your towel slung over your shoulder, you sip your drink, you smile at a stranger, and you are twelve again, only it's far better this second time around. Yes, it's true that there is an undercurrent of elitism in the Pines—New York gays are gay New Yorkers, after all. It helps to have youth or looks or money or all three, but don't let that stop you from enjoying the only place on earth that belongs completely to us.

Adjacent to the Pines is Cherry Grove, America's oldest lesbian retreat. It's also become a retreat for drag queens and booze-hounds. The Grove isn't as judgmental as the Pines: bodies aren't as sculpted (they may not be sculpted at all), and professional careers aren't as important. True to its bohemian roots, the Grove has got a far more laid-back feel than the Pines. For women, it's a place to be as butch or as femme as one might like. For men, the Grove is where to go if you like to sing show-tunes as you throw back your margaritas or howl at drag performers as you toss a few daiquiris. The Grove has a much more weathered, salty feel than the Pines, as well as a much greater sense of cultural democracy. Here you'll feel as far away from the pressures of Chelsea glamour as you would in a Fort Lauderdale dive bar. For some that's a blessing, for others a hellish nightmare.

Separating the Pines and the Grove is the Meatrack, a densely wooded intermediary zone that feels like it was planted by U.N. peacekeeping forces. And there might as well be a sign hanging from the trees that says, "Make Love, Not War." In fact, you're more likely to see signs that say, "Use Condoms or Die!" The Meatrack is cruising central. At all hours of the day—but especially at night—you'll find guys trolling for sex in the bushes of the Meatrack. When the bars close, the Meatrack opens. And if you get squeamish about public sex, the only other way to cross from the Pines to the Grove is to trek through the sand along the beach. It's kind of a semiofficial statement about the permanent role of public sex in gay culture. Some would say, if you don't like it, go straight.

Sand

Fire Island surely has some of the best beaches on the East Coast—clean, soft sand. But the best part is how easy the beach is to get to. No matter where you stay in the Pines or the Grove, you're never more than a two-minute walk from the ocean. And because the island is so secluded, it's fine to leave belongings—shoes, towels, groceries—at any of the boardwalk steps. The dunes are fragile, however, so it's important not to walk on them. And there can be a strong undertow. A few summers ago, we all watched in horror as rescue workers searched for a man who was pulled under. Alas, he was never found.

Chlorine

It's amazing to me the importance some guys place on having a pool in the Pines. Keep in mind, even the lowest-rent houses are no more than a few feet away from the ocean. And the beaches are some of the best in the U.S. We're talking wide stretches of near-white sand that last for miles.

So what's the obsession with having a pool? Well, as much as guys will claim to prefer the convenience of a private pool, I'm afraid it all comes down to one thing:

status. There's not that much to differentiate one Fire Island bungalow from another. You're not going to find a house with extra parking (there are no cars allowed on the island). You're probably not going to find one *without* outdoor showers or a hot tub. But a pool—now you're talking price differentials. Houses with pools rent for a lot more than those without. So if you want people to know that you're A-list, I guess a pool is *de rigueur*.

For my part, I have only one absolute rule on Fire Island: I need to be able to hear the soothing sound of the ocean from my porch. To me, that's all that matters. As long as I can hear the breaking of the waves, I can work on my novel or a play, knowing that I am in paradise. Then, when I have put in a few solid hours of writing, I can go for a dip in the sea, having earned my relaxation.

But hey, if a pool is what you want, go for it. It's just gonna cost you money.

Calories

Fire Island offers only a handful of eateries, none of them very good. Unlike the Hamptons, Fire Island isn't about dressing up or eating out. This is a place men come to express their domestic impulses. Pines kitchens are better stocked than most in the city. Since shopping on the island is limited (and expensive), most homeowners and house moms stock up on the mainland. But the Pines Pantry is the place to see and be seen at 4 o'clock as house groups pick up their salad greens, vegetables, fresh breads, and cheeses. Adjacent to the Pantry is a butcher shop (Peter's Meat Market), with a full range of meats and poultry items. (Note:

they don't take American Express). Wherever you stay, your housemates are sure to whip up an impressive meal (or expect you to). If you don't cook yourself, plan on doing some dishes. Fire Island may be the last place in America where families still have sit-down dinners every night.

Before dinner, those who aren't cooking will usually make their way to "Low Tea": cocktails on the pier. As the sun sets, "Low Tea" melds into "High Tea," which simply means the boys move upstairs to the deck. After dinner (most houses sit down to eat between 9 and 10 p.m.), everyone tromps off to the Pavilion for more drinks and (if you can stand the music) dancing.

There's not much "to do" on Fire Island. There are no movie theatres, no real shopping, no bookstores, no shows, etc. But people don't come to Fire Island to *do* anything. They come to lie on the beach, drink (and do drugs), eat, and hook up. It's gay life at its most basic. Those who prefer more active beach vacations—water-skiing, surfing, snorkeling, etc.—would do well to find another destination spot. Fire Island just isn't about do-ing; it's about *being*: being young, being pretty, being horny, being with friends, being in love, being mourn-ful over the end of a relationship, being drunk, being high—in a word, being gay.

Bar Tab

Evening activities on the Island follow a rigorous sched-ule and revolve around Tea Dance. Tea—so named be-cause it is a "light snack" that comes before the "real meal" of nighttime activities, just as tea time comes be-fore supper—is the Pines' most sacred institution. Tea begins every day at 6 p.m. (simply follow the crowds to the Pines pier). From 6 p.m. to 8 p.m., it is known as "Low Tea." Around 8 p.m., the boys move upstairs, at which point it becomes "High Tea." Since the drinks are weak and the prices exorbitant, most serious drinkers begin at home and arrive at Tea already buzzed. (For those in recovery—and those who should be—Fire Island has several AA and NA meetings a day).

Dinner on the island is usually eaten around 10 p.m. Someone in each house typically skips tea to make the repast.

After dinner, everyone heads back to the pier for dancing. There are essentially two dancing options: the Island Club, with no cover charge and pop beats, and the Pavilion, with a stiff cover charge and heavier club music. In recent years there has also been an underwear party held in the Grove. The party's organizers provide round-trip transportation for guys from the city to come out just for the affair. By dawn, the Pines boardwalks are crowded with guys stumbling back to their shares.

Over in the Grove, the schedule isn't nearly as rigid. Women head to Cherry's (58 Bayview Walk) and the Ice Palace (next to the Grove Hotel) or the Mostro, which stays open till dawn. Or they may grab a slice at Cherry Grove Pizza, have a meal at Rachel's, or dine at Top of the Bay.

Bedding (Shares)

A Fire Island house can rent for $10,000 a week, so few can afford to rent an entire house alone. Even a group of friends will be hard-pressed to pay for a house for the whole summer. As a result, Fire Island houses rent by the share. That means you rent a room (or more commonly, half a room) for a certain number of weeks each summer. It's helpful to know the lingo. A full share is the entire summer, from May to September, usually sixteen to eighteen weeks. A half share is ten to twelve alternating weeks, and a quarter share is four to five weeks (one week a month).

For half and quarter shares, houses will have an A-side and a B-side, meaning a room will flop back and forth between A and B from week to week. Don't be intimidated by the names. A isn't better than B or vice versa, unless you happen to like the dates of one side better than the other.

Each house has its own pricing plan for the A and B sides. If a side includes the big holiday weekends (Memorial Day, Pines Party, and Labor Day), expect to pay more. Some houses are far more flexible about weekend guests than others.

Every house has its own flavor, so it's a good idea to talk to someone who stayed in the house the summer before to find out what you're getting yourself into. I rented a share from an owner who claimed he would never be around. In fact, he was around constantly—arranging pillows, watering flowers, making sure we tidied up properly.

When you rent a share, in most cases you are actually renting your house from Thursday to Thursday. The majority of visitors come to Fire Island only for the weekend and arrive Thursday or Friday. But if you can take the time off, you're entitled to your house for the full week. It will be pretty quiet on the island Monday through Thursday, but it's also more intimate.

If you're looking for a share alone or with friends, and you live in New York, your best bet is one of the several share-a-thons held at the Gay and Lesbian Center in the spring. Otherwise, try Craigslist.

Bedding (Hotels)

Staying at a hotel on Fire Island should really be a last resort. Fire Island is not a place where people go out to eat or spend rainy afternoons shopping for tchotchkes. Island life revolves around dinner parties and dishing with friends. At the very least, try to meet a special someone who happens to have a share and could invite you over for a homemade meal.

The Hotel Ciel (Harbor Walk, Fire Island Pines). Few Pines partiers even realize that this cinder block building is actually a hotel; for most it just fades into the background of the pier's bar and dancing scene. It does boast one of the few restaurants in the Pines and has the only gym. Expect a two or three night minimum stay. Rates: $160–$200; Ph.: 631-597-6500, ext. 26; www.thepinesfireisland.com/pfihotel.html.

The Belvedere. Situated in Cherry Grove, this camp classic of a hotel has its own ballroom for those important black-tie soirés. Otherwise, don't expect to see the guests wearing anything at all. Despite being in the Grove, this is really a men's resort. Rates: $125–$500; Ph.: 631-597-6448; www.belvederefireisland.com.

The Madison Fire Island Pines. The Madison is a new guesthouse in the Pines offering such amenities as Wi-Fi and flat-screen TVs in every room. Rates: $200–$775; Ph.: 631-597-6061; www.themadisonfi.com.

Pines Paradise Bed-and-breakfast only has three rooms, so book early. Rates: $300–$500; Ph.: 212-368-7058 or 631-597-4130; Web: www.pinesparadise.com.

In and Out

Getting to Fire Island is almost as exciting as being there. You start in the bowels of Penn Station, take the

QUOTE

"In Cherry Grove I have seen young men earnestly studying Kropotkin, I have witnessed the arrival of Bella Abzug, campaigning, and of Della Reese, singing. I have seen witches, the usual good ones and bad ones. More than once I've encountered a mustachioed antebellum Southern belle wearing a pink and white hoop skirt."

—Gay writer Jack Nichols

A PERFECT DAY IN
THE PINES

A mug of coffee at the house and some pastry from the Pantry before anyone else gets up.

Writing a few pages while sitting on the deck.

A long stroll along the beach, down to the Grove and back.

Lunch from Pete's and the Pantry: a barbequed chicken, a bag of chips, and two cold cans of Diet Coke.

A few hours on the beach.

An outdoor shower with a new friend.

A frozen daiquiri prepared by a housemate.

A trip to the Pantry to pick up some last-minute items for dinner. Flirtatious smiles with someone you recognize from the beach.

A quick breeze through Low Tea.

A gourmet dinner with the housemates (with or without new friend).

A few more pages written.

An early night.

Long Island Rail Road to Sayville, grab one of the jam-packed shuttle buses to the ferry terminal, flaunt your new sunglasses while you're waiting on line for the ferry, and then be transported to gay Disneyland as you ride the magical ferry to the Pines or the Grove. Chances are you will arrive on a Friday evening and be greeted by tipsy revelers getting an early start on the weekend.

Ferry service back to Sayville (and train service back to Manhattan) is most frequent Sunday night and early Monday morning. There is usually a Monday express train that takes you right to Penn Station (it runs on Tuesdays after a big holiday). For ferry schedules, visit www.sayvilleferry.com. For train schedules, visit www.lirr.com.

It is also possible to drive to Sayville and park for the weekend at the train station or ferry terminal. Parking runs about $10 a day. There are no private cars allowed on Fire Island itself.

If you're feeling flush, you can take a water taxi, but expect to shell out the big bucks.

A Rainy Day in the Pines

Ugh. You've spent a lot of money on a share. You've brought your Armani sunglasses and swimsuit. And now its raining! Worst of all, in the Pines, there's *absolutely nothing to do.* No shopping, no movies, no theater. If you're lucky, your house or hotel will have a great video library. If not, you're basically out of luck. You can plan ahead, however, by bringing some flicks of your own. Below are some top camp classics, perfect for a rainy day. (For films actually set in Fire Island, see "Celluloid," at the end of the chapter).

Gay All the Way

The Boys in the Band. A 1970 classic with a dance
  number inspired by Tea in the Pines.

Making Love. Kate Jackson was the original deceived
wife and Harry Hamlin the original one-night stand.
Another Gay Movie. Okay, not a classic yet, but one of
the funniest, most outrageous movies ever made.

Diva Delights

Sunset Boulevard. A must for all gay men and their
friends.
Whatever Happened to Baby Jane. Perhaps the darkest
movie ever made about family relationships, but
beloved of gay men.
All About Eve. Bette Davis being Bette Davis.

Straight-But-Far-From-Narrow Seventies Science Fiction

Logan's Run. Everyone is young and beautiful in this
futuristic film because life is paradise till you turn
thirty—then it's time to die.
The Stepford Wives. The dark, edgy 1975 original that
was a serious indictment of a culture with constrain-
ing sex roles (all copies of the horrible 2004 remake
should be burned).
Soylent Green. A pointed, and slightly bizarre, commen-
tary on overpopulation.

Dinner in the Pines

Every gay man should know how to whip up a few simple items that will impress his housemates. Here are a
couple of summer recipes that will keep you off the bad
boy list. Fire Island cooking is a team sport, so you

won't have to cook alone. Still, even when you team up with someone more comfortable in the kitchen, it's nice to have a few recipes to call your own.

Mojitos for Six

20 fresh mint sprigs
¼ cup sugar
1 cup plus 2 tbsp fresh lime juice
1 cup plus 2 tbsp light rum
club soda (chilled)
ice
6 slices of lime

In a small bowl, crush the mint with the back of a spoon, then, as best you can, spread the mint inside six tall glasses to coat the inside of each glass. In a pitcher, mix the sugar and lime juice and stir thoroughly. Add the rum and mix. Fill each glass with ice and divide the mojito mixture evenly among the glasses. Top off with the club soda. Add a lime slice to each glass, and serve.

Steak au Poivre for Six
Most houses on Fire Island have a grill (and someone who knows how to use it). I have adapted this traditional pan sauté recipe accordingly.

3 tbsp black peppercorns
6 boneless shell steaks (¾ pound each, about 1¼ inches thick)
3 tbsp butter

3 tbsp vegetable oil
6 shallots, sliced
¼ cup heavy cream
6 tbsp Cognac or brandy

In a heavy-duty sealable plastic bag or between two sheets of wax paper, crush peppercorns with the bottom of a heavy skillet. Pat the steaks dry and coat all sides with the crushed peppercorn. Cook the steaks on the grill, four to five minutes on each side for medium rare. Season steaks with salt and transfer to plates.

Heat butter and oil in skillet until melted and sizzling. Pour in red juices from steak plate. Add shallots and cook till they turn clear. Add cream and Cognac. Keep heating until sauce thickens and coats back of spoon, about 1 minute. Season sauce with salt and spoon over steaks.

Summer Salad
Serves 6–8

Salad is about balancing color and texture. This salad is light and refreshing. The key is Boston lettuce. Don't substitute romaine or you'll get a salad that is too heavy, and don't use iceberg or you'll have housemates snickering behind your back.

3 heads Boston lettuce
3 yellow peppers
3 red peppers
about 20 cherry tomatoes

For the dressing:

¾ cup olive oil
¼ cup freshly squeezed lemon juice
1 tbsp dijon mustard

Wash and dry the lettuce. Cut the peppers into squares. Halve the tomatoes. Toss all the vegetables together. Combine the dressing ingredients in a bowl. Toss with the salad just prior to serving.

Lemon Mousse
The perfect summer dessert.

6 egg yolks
1 cup sugar
juice of four lemons
2 cups whipping cream

Combine the egg yolks, sugar, and lemon juice in a saucepan and heat over a low flame, stirring constantly. When the lemon-curd mixture begins to boil, heat for about a minute more, then set aside to cool. Whip the cream till it forms stiff peaks. Fold in the lemon curd, then spoon into glasses and chill. Your housemates will be charmed.

Pages

At one extreme, Esther Newton's *Cherry Grove, Fire Island: Sixty Years in America's First Gay and Lesbian Town* is a serious, scholarly history of the Grove. At the other extreme, James English's *Escape from Fire Island!* is a mystery modeled on the *Choose Your Own Adventure* series we loved when we were kids. In between is Felice Picano's *A House on the Ocean, a House on the Bay*, which is supposed to be a literary memoir, but reads more like an unedited diary from the 1980s. If you don't mind a bit of a downer, John Jiler's *Dark Wind* is a nonfiction account of the 1985 hurricane that hit Fire Island at the height of the AIDS crisis.

Jack Nichols's *Welcome to Fire Island: Visions of Cherry Grove and the Pines* is now out of print but was once a classic primer for first-time visitors to the island. Larry Kramer's once-controversial *Faggots* was inspired by his 1970s experiences in the Pines. By far the best literary account of life on the Island, however, is to be found in Ethan Mordden's collection of short stories known as the "Buddies cycle."

Celluloid

Below are a few film faves set on Fire Island:

Longtime Companion (1990). A major motion picture about a group of friends dealing with the impact of AIDS.

Boys in the Sand (1971). A porn film made by once well-known director Wakefield Poole and starring Casey Donovan. In the seventies, the line between "art" and "porn" was just being drawn, so *Boys in the Sand* was actually reviewed in some mainstream newspapers.

The Meatrack: Confessions of a Male Hustler. A 1970 film now available on DVD from Something Weird

Video. It comes on the same DVD with "Sticks and Stones," a short film set at a 4th of July Fire Island Party. From the case: "Two very different but equally nostalgic time capsules of the 1970 Gay Scene, full of love, lust and naked butts."

Boy friends on Rehoboth Beach.

CHAPTER FOUR

Relaxing in Rehoboth

WHEN WAS THE LAST TIME you had a pink peppermint ice cream cone? Or a bucket of freshly made caramel corn? Or savored a piece of chewy saltwater taffy—the kind that sticks in your teeth? If it's been a while—and not just because you're on a low-carb diet—it's time to go to Rehoboth Beach.

I'll admit I have a certain fondness for Rehoboth simply because we spent so many summers there as a family when I was growing up. And it is still the quintessential boardwalk-and-beach town, complete with a Fun Time amusement park, multiple arcades featuring video games and skeet-ball lanes, and all those saltwater taffy shops. But over the past few decades, Rehoboth has developed a second identity—as DC's official gay getaway.

The first thing you'll notice as you drive into Rehoboth (or arrive by the Rehobus, which leaves regularly from Adams Morgan in Washington, DC), is what's missing. They surround you while you're still on Route 1, but as soon as you enter Rehoboth you won't see them: McDonalds, Burger King, KFC, Starbucks,

Delaware has no sales tax, making it a favorite destination of serious shoppers.

the Gap, J Crew, or any of the other chain stores that have metastasized across the national landscape. Nor will you be bombarded with tackiness as in Fort Lauderdale or Key West. Instead, on Rehoboth Avenue you will be treated to the sight of The Ice Cream Store and dozens of other mom-and-pop stores, some of them in business since the 1910s.

Rehoboth was founded back in the 1880s as a Christian community. It still has an air of absolute wholesomeness. Well, sort of. In the last twenty years a second Rehoboth has developed, offering gay guesthouses, gay bars, gay restaurants, and gay shops. In Rehoboth, gays and straights live parallel lives. Literally. The straights along Rehoboth Avenue, the gays along Baltimore Avenue, the two streets running parallel to each other.

Rehoboth Avenue is the street you see as you enter town. It is the one lined with all the sweet shops and family-owned pizza joints. Its colors are sedate: blue, white, gray—imitating the sea, the sand, and the boardwalk. Here you'll see strollers and smiling parents, giggling teenage girls, and preening teenage boys. One block away is Baltimore Avenue. Here the architecture is more colorful—reds, yellows, and oranges vie for attention. The street life is more colorful, too, as virtually everyone on Baltimore is gay. There's a gay bookstore, gay swimsuit shops, gay bars, gay restaurants, etc.

Rehoboth is a marriage of convenience. The gays stay off Rehoboth Avenue and the straights stay off Baltimore. When I mentioned to a local that I planned on heading over to Rehoboth Avenue to get a bite to eat, she looked at me like I'd lost my mind. Perhaps it's out of respect for the families who come to Rehoboth Avenue for light summer fun (and tax-free shopping) or out of genuine revulsion for the straight world, but the Baltimore Avenue gays are perfectly content to live on their own separate street. But the town's commitment to pluralism runs deep. The name Rehoboth is, in fact, a biblical word meaning "a place for all."

According to local legend, Rehoboth's gay origins date back to the 1920s, when Louisa du Pont Carpenter used to throw glamorous parties at her mansion on the beach (not far from where the gay section—Poodle Beach—lies now). Hollywood types would fly in for the occasion (the Du Ponts had their own private airstrip) and all sorts of goings-on would take place. Rehoboth soon earned a reputation as a secret getaway for Hollywood's closeted gays. In the forties and fifties, this meant clandestine dinner parties in people's homes, but it was better than nothing. In the sixties, a gay bar opened on the boardwalk—the Pink Pony—but there was a local law prohibiting pedestrian movement while in possession of an alcoholic beverage. This meant it was illegal to walk around a bar with a drink in one's hand. While no officer was going to enforce such a law in a straight bar, in a gay one, it could serve as a pretext for a raid. So gay patrons at the Pink Pony would sit at the bar and talk only to those at barstools to their left and right.

The Pink Pony was destroyed by a flood, but in the 1970s attitudes were relaxing faster than ice cream melts on a hot day. The disco craze and sexual liberation hit Rehoboth as they hit everywhere else. The Nomad Village opened just outside Rehoboth. It not only had dancing, it had a backroom for sexual mingling.

In 1980 the first gay-owned restaurant opened in town—the Back Porch. It was an upscale establishment, but it was burned down. Tensions mounted in the early nineties when all of America was caught between the fervor of evangelical Christianity and the sexual libertarianism of Madonna. The Strand, a gay bar, opened right on Rehoboth Avenue, the town's main strip. The town had a brief paroxysm of homophobia. Bumper stickers appeared declaring "Keep Rehoboth a Family Town." In response, local activists formed CAMP ("Create a More Positive") Rehoboth. They worked behind the scenes to improve relations with the town's political leadership. As more and more gays and lesbians bought property, the mood settled. By the late nineties, Rehoboth was officially a gay mecca. Today it is "on the circuit," and in summer, dance parties will draw thousands. Even if you're not into the circuit scene, when you've had your fill of

Community leaders say that the majority of Rehoboth's gay summer visitors are male, while the majority of gay property owners are female.

sunbathing, you'll probably be in the mood for a House Party. True to the town's open spirit, Rehoboth House Parties are unusually welcoming affairs. They are often advertised in the *Camp Rehoboth Newsletter* and all are invited.

Just off the main drag, Rehoboth is an all-American town, with colonial-style homes and sidewalks lined with oak trees. Lawns are perfectly manicured and American flags are everywhere. But so are gay pride flags, which gives the town a quirky Jefferson-in-Paris feel. It is much more clean-cut than Provincetown; even though Delaware is north of the Mason-Dixon line, there's a distinctly Southern sensibility. Nudity on the beaches is strictly taboo. I was told a story about two female tourists who insisted on going topless—even after being told that local laws prohibited it. The two women got into an altercation with the police. When the police won, and the two women grudgingly donned their tops, the surrounding gays applauded—for the police. Toto, I don't think we're in the Pines anymore.

Sand

The main gay beach is Poodle Beach. Take a right at the boardwalk and keep walking about a mile till you see rainbow flags instead of families. A beautiful stretch of sand, Poodle Beach is one of the rare gay beaches in the U.S. to have chairs and umbrellas conveniently for rent ($5 for a chair, $7 for an umbrella). Volleyball is a popular pastime at Poodle, with a drag tournament on Labor Day Sunday that draws confused crowds of gays and straights alike. Sunbathers in Rehoboth tend to cluster together, so don't be surprised if you take a nap only to wake up and find someone has placed his blanket a few millimeters from yours.

Women tend to head for the North Shores beach in the state park, about 2 miles from town. Expect something of a trek.

Calories

The gays love their high-end restaurants, and Rehoboth has plenty to choose from. Some top picks: Eden (23 Baltimore Ave.; 302-227-3330). Eden is a favorite of the critics with fresh fish, dry aged Angus beef, and wild game.

59 Lake (59 Lake Ave.; 302-226-5900). Arguably the town's hottest restaurant. Ross Fraser is 59 Lake's celebrity chef.

Fusion (50 Wilmington Ave., 302-226-1940). Not my kind of cuisine, but another darling of the critics. Chef-owner Jonathan Spivak plays with gastronomic combinations from around the world.

While it's possible to eat only at critically acclaimed, gourmet restaurants while in Rehoboth, indulge at least once in some of the boardwalk's lesser-than-haute cuisine. See Rehoboth's Boardwalk Bests, below, for some suggestions.

Bedding

Like the Pines, Rehoboth is a house-share town. Most guys from DC and Philadelphia will pool their resources and organize a share for the summer. Fortunately, however, there are also plenty of other options. Don't expect luxury in Rehoboth, though, as most of the "inns" have a motel feel.

The Shore Inn (703 Rehoboth Ave.). Just a little too far from the beach to be truly convenient, the Shore Inn nevertheless has its own pool, hot tub, video library, frisky houseboys, and afternoon social hour. Rates: $130–$235; Ph.: 800-597-8899; www.shoreinn.com.

At Melissa's (36 Delaware Ave). One and a half blocks from the ocean and only two blocks from Rehoboth Avenue, this bed-and-breakfast is definitely well located. Relax on the porch or throw your own BBQ in the back yard (the grill is for guests' use); you will feel like you are at your best girlfriend's beach house. Rates: $210–$245; Ph.: 800-396-8090; www.atmelissas.com.

The Rehoboth Guesthouse (40 Maryland Ave.) is a gay-owned bed-and-breakfast close to the ocean. There are two decks for sunbathing in case you don't feel like heading to the beach, but this is NOT a clothing-optional resort. Saturday afternoon wine-and-cheese parties are hosted by the staff. Rates: $95–$205; Ph.: 800-564-0493; www.rehobothguesthouse.com.

Bar Tab

True to its Methodist origins, Rehoboth is an early town. Don't bother looking for the megaclubs, you won't find them, but circuit parties do occasionally come to town.

The Blue Moon (35 Baltimore Ave.) has a busy happy hour and frequent drag shows.

The Purple Parrot (247 Rehoboth Ave.) has a Sunday night drag show right on Rehoboth Ave. that attracts gays and straights alike.

59 Lake (59 Lake Ave.) is a restaurant that converts into a dance club.

Aqua Grill (57 Baltimore Ave.) gets a large, early evening crowd.

In and Out

By car, Rehoboth is 130 miles from Washington, DC, and 230 miles from New York. From either city you take I-95 till you hit Route 1, then bear south.

Parking in Rehoboth is a hassle. Rehoboth and Baltimore Avenue meters are in effect from 10 a.m. until midnight and the rate is $1.00 an hour. If you need change, there are machines at First St. and Rehoboth Ave. and on the third block of Rehoboth Ave. (on the island across from city hall).

It's probably worth your while to pick up a parking permit, as you will need one to park anywhere near the beach. A weekend permit costs $10 a day (or $20 for three days). You can pick up a parking permit at City Hall (229 Rehoboth Ave.), at the Parking Meter Division (301/2 Lake Ave.), at various real estate offices in

REHOBOTH'S
BOARDWALK BESTS

Best Pizza: Louie's (11 Rehoboth Ave.)

Best Fries: Thrashers (26 Rehoboth Ave.)

Best Soft Serve Chocolate and Vanilla Twist: Nice
Cream Day (42 Rehoboth Ave.)

Best Selection of Flavors: The Ice Cream Store (6
Rehoboth Ave.) Try the Amaretto Garlic, but
skip the Vanilla and Bacon.

Best Fried Chicken: Gus & Gus's (15 South
Boardwalk—right on the beach)

town, and right on Rehoboth Avenue as you come into
town (look for someone selling them by the side of the
road).

If you're staying relatively close to the beach, you
won't need a car in Rehoboth, unless it rains and you
yearn to head to the malls for some tax-free shopping.

The Rehobus

The gay-owned Rehobus provides round-trip bus service from DC's Adams Morgan. It was originally intended to be a gay bus service—and male models serve
as hosts on board—but in practice it turns out to draw a

Q FACT

No one knows for sure how saltwater taffy got its name, but the most popular legend says it all began when a shop selling taffy was flooded with ocean water during a major storm in 1883. Not knowing what to do with the soaked candy, the store owner began marketing it as saltwater taffy.

mixed crowd. Buses depart from a variety of locations, so check the Web site for details. Don't worry, this isn't Trailways. Rehobus coaches come equipped with flat-screen HD monitors, DVD players, satellite TV, and XM radio. Each seat has its own plug-in for headphones, and you can choose from six channels of XM radio, or watch various video selections. There are also outlets to plug in your computer. Regulars congregate at the Duplex Diner before Friday evening departures for pre-trip drinks. You can also order meals in advance through the diner and have them provided to you on board. 888-MY RHBUS (888-697-4287); www.rehobus .com.

Pages

Fay Jacobs is Rehoboth's unofficial chronicler of gay and lesbian life along the mid-Atlantic shore. *As I Lay Frying: A Rehoboth Beach Memoir* recounts Jacobs's arrival in Rehoboth and her decision to settle in the community. In *Fried and True: Tales from Rehoboth Beach*, she continues her autobiographical account of beach living. You will often find Jacobs signing books near the offices of CAMP Rehoboth on Baltimore Avenue.

Key West's main port.

CHAPTER FIVE

South Florida: Some Like It Hot

"The two basic items necessary to sustain life are sunshine and coconut milk. Did you know that? That's a fact. In Florida, they got a terrific amount of coconut trees there."

—Ratso in *Midnight Cowboy* (1969)

FLORIDA EVOKES contradictory images—grandparents in retirement homes, college students on spring break, art deco revival, tacky strip malls. For gays and lesbians, Florida remains a movable feast. Once upon a time, gays were loyal to Key West, with its bohemian flair and home-at-the-end-of-the-world vibe. Then gays discovered—and transformed—Miami Beach, turning it into one of the most chic resorts in the world. But nothing can stay chic forever, and soon the gays were venturing farther north, into that most hallowed of college student ground: Fort Lauderdale. Now, Fort Lauderdale is a veritable queer resort destination, even though it has neither the charm of Key West nor the sex appeal of South Beach. But in Fort Lauderdale it's possible to visit one's grandmother *and* find love on the beach, so that's something, right? Still, if you're headed to Florida, skipping Miami is like skipping the Magic Kingdom: okay if you've been at least once before, otherwise practically unpatriotic. Fortunately, the drive between Fort Lauderdale and South Beach should take you no more than an hour. Avoid South Florida in the summertime—the heat is simply cruel. Moreover, hurricane season starts June 1 and runs through November. Statistically speaking, August and September are the two months most affected by major storms in the Atlantic basin.

South Beach (SoBe)

There aren't many places where you can sit at a beachside café and watch the models go by, where you can get a good night's sleep and then go dancing at 6 a.m., where you can admire art deco buildings as they *should* have been painted. Still, the raw sensuality of Miami can be a little overwhelming.

These days, South Beach is known as a Latino lover's paradise. It's often said that one of the great things about being in South Beach is that it's almost like being in the United States. How did this tiny piece of

South Florida become, for a brief period at the end of the twentieth century, one of the most cosmopolitan parts of the entire country? Well, consider the fact that the one-and-a-half square mile district is entirely free from the monstrous high-rises that tower over the rest of South Florida. That alone gives South Beach a distinctive, welcoming feel. But there was a time when South Beach wasn't welcoming at all. At least, not to anyone other than the elderly and the criminal.

But while the thugs who ruled Miami in the 1980s fostered a culture of drugs and violence, the quiet arrival of the gays led to an architectural revival like none other. When gay interior designer Leonard Horowitz repainted the district's peeling art deco buildings in brilliant pastels and added tasteful hints of neon, he transformed the city into a living sound-stage. Not surprisingly, the cameras soon arrived and the hit television show *Miami Vice* was born. South Beach had everything a television director could want: vibrant backdrops, constant drug wars, and perfect weather to show off buff bodies. Soon enough, the last remaining elderly folks were priced out, crime was curtailed, the modeling agencies moved in, and celebrities started opening restaurants with "no reservations" policies. By the early 1990s, Gianni Versace had virtually claimed South Beach as his own personal estate, Ian Schrager had basically appointed himself mayor, and Madonna was, for all intents and purposes, the town's patron saint. Which, needless to say, made it a very exciting place to be. Once the annual White Party began, South Beach was officially a gay mecca. Versace's murder in 1997, Schrager's subsequent expansion into a global brand name, and Madonna's foray into motherhood sapped South Beach of some of its previous vitality. Still, it's worth a visit, if only to see the town almost every supermodel in the world once called "home."

Bedding

In South Beach, there's no need to stay at a gay hotel. In fact, you'll have a hard time finding one. But all the hotels are gay friendly, and you can find some great deals at the smaller, art deco places right on the beach. All rates are for high season (October through April).

The Clay (1438 Washington St.). One of the best deals in the nation. Part hostel, part hotel. Not as cheap as it once was, but still an unbelievable find. Some people wouldn't dream of staying anywhere that could be construed as a youth hostel, but the Clay, with its wooden ceiling fans and numerous balcony alcoves, will transport you to another time and place. Rates: $75–$226; Ph.: 305-534-2988; www.clayhotel.com.

Jefferson House (1018 Jefferson Ave.). Jefferson House is close enough to the beach to be convenient, just far enough away from the action to offer a restful night's sleep. When you don't feel like dealing with the beach scene, you can always relax by the Jefferson House pool. Rates: $175–$345; Ph.: 877-599-5247; www .jeffersonhouse.com.

Avalon (700 Ocean Dr.). Sometimes it's nice to be right in the heart of the action. At the Avalon you're on the beach and in the thick of it all. Think simple, stream-lined rooms. Rates: $200–$500; Ph.: 800-933-3306; www.avalonhotel.com.

Hotel Victor (114 Ocean Dr). If you have money to burn, the Hotel Victor offers boutique-style luxury and prime views of the gay beach. Not a gay hotel per se (it's owned by Hyatt), but definitely attracts a sophisticated gay clientele and is gay friendly. The Web site is ex-tremely annoying, so you might as well call. Rates: $608–$1600; Ph.: 305-428-1234; www.hotelvictorsouthbeach .com.

The Delano (1685 Collins Ave.). Once upon a time, you could sneak through the hotel's Philippe Stark-designed Alice in Wonderland lobby and get to the heavenly pool area. But guards (dressed immaculately in white) now make that impossible. Not the kind of hotel where you can kick back and relax, but one that you will never forget. Rates: Very expensive, call for details; Ph.: 800-848-1775; www.delano-hotel .com.

Sand

Head to 12th Street and Ocean Drive. Miami's gay beach is one of the most accessible (if also one of the most snooty) in the world. Miami Beach has famously white sand, though it is rapidly disappearing and there is some talk of importing sand from afar. The water temperature is moderate. Don't forget to pack your Armani swimsuit and steroids.

Bar Tab

South Beach is all about what's hot now, so you're going to have to do some research if you want to be hip. If you really want trendy, your best bet may be to find someone beautiful and well dressed and stalk them from a safe distance till you end up at the club of the hour. Actual gay bars are almost nonexistent, but the entire South Beach district has a gay air. Alas, drugs are rampant, which means so are fights and ugly scenes. Twist (1057 Washington Ave.) is a South Beach institution and the closest thing SoBe has to a locals bar. Score (727 Lincoln Rd) has both food and dancing. A blend of café, bar, and dance club, Laundry Bar (721 North Lincoln Lane) is the place to go if you're thirsty and you need to do a load (of laundry). B.E.D.

Q HINT

When MapQuesting destinations to/from South Beach, be sure to enter the city as "Miami Beach"; otherwise you are likely to be given directions for Key Biscane or downtown Miami itself.

(929 Washington Ave.) is, yes, another one of those places that has beds instead of couches. It draws a mixed crowd. Twilo (30 NE 11th St.) is outside the South Beach Art Deco District, in Miami proper. It's a standard circuit-music club.

Calories

In the 1990s, South Beach established itself as a capital of international cuisine. Restaurants tend to be expensive and you'll have to check the fashion magazines for the latest celebrity-chef openings.

The cafés along Ocean—including the News Café (800 Ocean Dr.), the Pelican (826 Ocean Dr.), and Mango's (900 Ocean Dr.)—are all convenient places to watch the Latin boys go by. Mark's at the Hotel Nash (1120 Collins) is celebrity chef-owner Mark Militello's contribution to SoBe cuisine. Expect to pay for the privilege of eating here.

China Grill (404 Washington Ave.) is a true groundbreaker in fusion—your credit card gets fused to the bill. Front Porch Café (424 Ocean): Wake up from a night of partying and enjoy breakfast at the Front Porch. .the same idea. Joe's Stone Crab (11 Washington Ave.). There's nothing hip about Joe's Stone Crab, but the food is good and draws a constant crowd.

In and Out

Miami International Airport is approximately 20 minutes from South Beach; Fort Lauderdale International Airport is closer to an hour. A car in South Beach is a major hassle and you won't need one anyway, unless you intend to head up to Fort Lauderdale or the nude beach at Haulover. In which case, splurge and rent a convertible.

NUDE SUNBATHING IN SOUTH FLORIDA

If you feel an urge to skinny-dip or just want to escape the oppressively perfect bodies of South Beach, head north by car to Haulover, Miami's "official" nude beach. From Miami, take Collins Avenue north till you get to Bal Bay Drive (about 20 minutes). Park in the North parking lot, which will be on your left. When you cross over to the beach, go to your left to reach the boys' section.

JULIA: Having three-way sex in my house is a very big deal, Matt.

MATT: You guys are lucky that that was all I was doing. I know kids hooked on crank, kids who are plotting to blow up the school.

JULIA: Congratulations. You win the award for least screwed-up teenager.

—from *Nip/Tuck*, a sitcom set in Miami ("Cliff Mantegna," Season 1)

Fort Lauderdale

Personally, I still find it hard to believe that Fort Lauderdale has become such a major gay destination. I have too many memories of rushing with my grandparents to catch the earlybird special—at 4 p.m. As we ate, my grandmother would pocket rolls in her purse, "In case you get hungry later. I'm paying for them. Why should they go to waste?!" Then again, when I was very little I liked coming here because no one ever seemed busy in Fort Lauderdale. Even the grown-ups spent their time playing games (after all, what's really more fun than an evening of bingo?). Maybe that's what we all still like about it. Fort Lauderdale says a loud "no" to the Protestant work ethic of delayed gratification—which is why it has always held special appeal to Jewish retirees, partying college students, and beach bums.

Fort Lauderdale has one of the longest stretches of beach in North America—23 miles to be exact—but the gay beach takes up a relatively small section at the corner of Sebastian Street and A1A.

Though lacking in charm, Fort Lauderdale has become a center of gay life. In fact, an estimated half million gays visit every year. There's even an entirely gay shopping mall. Perhaps because Fort Lauderdale lacks the aesthetic appeal of its sister city, South Beach, it has

Q FACT

Wilton Manors, adjacent to Fort Lauderdale proper, was the second city in the country to elect a gay-majority city council (the first was West Hollywood).

a far more relaxed and democratic air. You can leave your Prada shoes at home. That means less costly venues and much cheaper fare. But don't expect to feel like one of the fabulous. Fort Lauderdale is just this side of tacky.

If you're craving sophistication, but can't afford to get out of town, your best bet is to head to Las Olas Boulevard, Fort Lauderdale's (Disneyesque) version of Fifth Avenue. An even better idea is to see elegance in its natural state at the Flamingo Gardens, where you can see hot-pink birds with attitude (3750 South

FORT LAUDERDALE'S MACHO MAYOR

In 2007, the mayor of Fort Lauderdale, Jim Naugle, garnered the wrath of the gay community when he proposed that the city spend $250,000 on a robotic toilet for the beach to reduce "homosexual activity" in public restrooms. To make matters worse, he told the press that he used the term "homosexual" rather than "gay" because, in his estimation, homosexuals were "unhappy." A variety of other public statements pitted him directly against Fort Lauderdale's gay population.

Alas, Florida has a history of antigay activism. It was in Dade county in 1976 that actress Anita Bryant launched her now-infamous movement to roll back gay rights under the banner of protecting children.

Flamingo Road, www.flamingogardens.org). Generally speaking, however, the gay neighborhoods of Fort Lauderdale are Victoria Park and Wilton Manors.

Bedding (Gay)

With a few notable exceptions, most gay guesthouses in Fort Lauderdale match the overall tenor of the town: as cheap as Chinet and just as tacky. Expect plenty of pictures of nude men—and plenty of live nude men too. You'd have to dig deep into the sand to find a Fort Lauderdale guesthouse that isn't "clothing optional." Even the most luxurious properties have a highly charged sexual ambience. All rates are high season.

Coconut Grove Guesthouse (3012 Grenada St.) bills itself as "the gay guesthouse closest to the beach," but we're talking a difference of inches, not feet. The best thing about this property is not the location but the architecture: built in 1939, the three-story plantation-style building has wooden verandas and louvered doors, giving it a Key West ambience. Clothing optional with pool and Jacuzzi. Rates: $165–$300; Ph.: 888-414-3226; www.cococuntgroveguesthouse.com.

Coral Reef Guesthouse (2609 NE 13th St.). Offers a clothing-optional atmosphere, pool and Jacuzzi. Rates: $95–$225; Ph.: 954-568-0292; www.coralreefguesthouse .com.

Dunes Guesthouse (2835 Terramar St.). Formerly the Saint Sebastian, and reopened by the owners of the Dunes in Saugatuck, MI. Clothing-optional pool area with "al fresco breakfast." (Whether you wish to have your breakfast while unclothed is up to you.) Rates: $154–$1891; Ph.: 954-568-6161; www.dunesguesthouse .com.

Windamar Beach Resort (543 Breakers Ave.). From the Web site: "The Windamar is one of the few truly clothing-optional properties in Fort Lauderdale. We don't just offer nude swimming or clothing-optional areas, our entire resort is comfortable and private for the true nudist or naturalist. We like to think of ourselves as a clothing-tolerated resort, not just clothing optional!" Rates: $149–$199; Ph.: 800-554-6816; www .windamarbeachresort.com.

Luxurious yet clothing-optional, the award-winning Royal Palms Resort (2901 Terramar St.) is the quintessential gay hotel. The resort's rooms feature such name-brand amenities as Frette sheets (320 thread count, to be exact), Hansgrohe showerheads, and Bose CD players. Here you'll feel equally comfortable in your $500 Prada swimsuit or in nothing at all. Rates: $259–$359; Ph.: 800-237-7256; www.royalpalms.com.

Another clothing-optional retreat with award-winning accommodations is the beautiful Pineapple Point Guesthouse (315 N.E. 16th Terrace). Rates: $289–$559; Ph.: 888-844-7295; www.pineapplepoint.com.

Bedding (Not So Gay)

Traditional hotels in Fort Lauderdale are starting to gain in style (and price). One nice, if expensive, alternative to the large chains and sketchy properties that dot the coast is The Atlantic (601 N. Fort Lauderdale Beach Blvd.), an upscale boutique hotel with perfect

views. Rates: $250–$800; Ph.: 954-567-8020; www
.starwood.com/luxury.

Calories

Canyon Southwest Café (1818 East Sunrise Blvd.; 954-765-1950; www.canyonfl.com) isn't cheap but has good Southwestern cuisine. Hi Life Café (3000 N. Federal Hwy.; 954-563-1395; www.hilifecafe.com) is worth a visit simply because owner-chef Carlos Fernandez was a "Top Chef" contestant in 2006.

Rosie's Bar & Grill is conveniently located to the gay shops and streets of Wilton Manors. For a late-night snack, head to Lester's Diner (250 State Road 84) where you will be transported back to the 1950s—whether you like it or not.

Swamp Water Café, about half an hour by car from Fort Lauderdale on the Big Cypress Reservation, specializes in, yes, swamp food: alligator nuggets, frog legs, etc. Galanga (2389 Wilton Dr., Wilton Manors; 954-202-0000) is where the gays go for Asian food. Expect a crowd and book a reservation in advance.

Sand

The gay section of Fort Lauderdale's endless beach can be found at the intersection of Sebastian Street and A1A (A1A runs along the coast). A second, less popular beach begins at NE 18th. Fort Lauderdale's beach is deservedly famous for its miles of golden sand, but because it lacks the geographical features that make other beaches more interesting, it has a certain bland quality. Even in Florida, the water of the Atlantic tends to be cold.

Haulover, the nude beach, is located 30 minutes south. Take A1A south till it becomes Collins Ave. Haulover Beach is located at approximately 10800 Collins Ave. Park in the North parking lot, which will be on your left. When you cross over to the beach, go to your left to reach the boys' section.

Bar Tab

Those who like to drink will be very happy in Fort Lauderdale, where bars are almost as plentiful as palm trees. Most of the bars live in what are essentially gay strip malls. What the clubs lack in glamour, they make up for in cheap drinks.

Boardwalk (1721 N. Andrews Ave.) is a popular strip club with an outdoor patio. Boom (2232 Wilton Dr.) and George's Alibi (2266 Wilton Dr.) feature regular drink specials. The Cubby Hole (823 N. Federal Highway) is for bears. Jackhammer (1727 N. Andrews Extension) and Ramrod (1508 NE 4th Ave., Wilton Manors) are Fort Lauderdale's leather/Levi's bars. The Ramrod sponsors events such as Fetish Fridays, Caged Saturdays, Leather Sundays, and Hot Ash Cigar Night on Thursdays. For dancing, head to Steel (1951 N.W. Powerline Ave).

Fort Lauderdale also has two lesbian bars: New Moon (2440 Wilton Dr.) in Wilton Manors and Beach Betty's (625 E. Dania Beach Blvd.)

In and Out

Fort Lauderdale/Hollywood International Airport is about twenty minutes from downtown Fort Lauderdale.

Miami International Airport is closer to an hour. You will need to rent a car in Fort Lauderdale, as distances between locations tend to be great. If you're in a pinch, the Tri-Rail from Miami airport to Fort Lauderdale is only $5 per person, and you could theoretically take cabs around town.

Key West

Key West is one of those places that every gay person ought to visit at least once. Like San Francisco, Key West is a town where gays and straights live as if they never got the memo that we're supposed to distrust one another. Perhaps that's because in mellowed-out Key West, no one has ever gotten (or at least bothered to read) a memo about anything.

Key West is not the gay mecca it once was. Now that we're almost fully integrated into our national melting pot, maybe we feel less of a need to find ref-

QUOTE

"Always do sober what you said you'd do drunk. That will teach you to keep your mouth shut."

—Erstwhile Key West resident
Ernest Hemingway

uge by traveling as far south as we can go without crossing the border. But even if Key West is less queer than in its glory days, it's good to know that places like it exist, where you can drop out of mainstream American life without even having to learn another language (though a few words of Spanish wouldn't hurt if you want to get your café con leche from one of the local bodegas).

Ironically, Key West has no real beach. Locals will act befuddled if you ask them how to get to the sand. Gays therefore congregate poolside at the town's numerous, clothing-optional guesthouses.

Most people who frequent Key West do so because they've fallen in love with its subtropical pace and eclectic mix of architectural styles. Key West is the southernmost isle in the chain known as the Florida Keys. It practically touches Cuba, which accounts for the brisk sale of Cuban cigars along Duval Street.

Key West's origins as a queer sort of town date back to the 1860s, when it was populated mainly by treasure hunters, smugglers, and their well-paid lady friends. It was rediscovered a century later in the 1960s by writers, artists, and joint-smoking hippies. The gays started coming en masse in the seventies. Today, gays make up a third of the population (the town actually elected an openly gay mayor way back in 1983). More recently, Key West has attracted the cruise-ship crowd and a growing number of college students on spring break.

Bedding

Alexander's (1118 Fleming St.). A little far afield, Alexander's is nevertheless a solid choice for those who want a house with a low sexual temperature. Have a glass of complimentary lemonade by the pool. Welcoming to both gays and lesbians. Rates: $115–$365; Ph. 800-654-9919 or 305-294-9919; www.alexanderskeywest .com.

Big Ruby's Guesthouse (409 Appelrouth Lane). In the heart of town, and a great place for singles because of the early-evening mixers (and even some occasional dinner parties). Rates: $165–$549; Ph.: 800-477-7829 or 305-296-2323; www.bigrubys.com.

The Oasis, the Coconut Grove, and the Coral Tree Inn (815–823 Fleming St.). Don't expect luxury, but you will make new friends at this male-only complex of guesthouses. Rates: $139–$289; Ph. 800-362-7477; www .oasiskeywest.com.

Equator (818 Fleming St.) has a sophisticated ambience, but you'll find most of the guests wearing only

THE KEY WEST CALENDAR

Mid-May: Pride Festival

June: Gay arts festival

September: Women's festival

October: Fantasy Fest (features Masked Madness, the Headdress Ball, and the Pet Masquerade)

Last Saturday of October: Twilight Parade (attracts upwards of 50,000 spectators)

their birthday suits. There's a two-person outdoor shower for your enjoyment. Rates: $120–$230; Ph. 800-278-4552 or 305-294-7775; www.equatorresort.com.

Island House (1129 Fleming St.) is a cross between an upscale hotel and a sex club. Rates: $95–$499; Ph. 800-890-6284; www.islandhousekeywest.com.

Pearl's Rainbow (525 United St.). A clothing-optional women's retreat. Rates: $99–$369; Ph. 800-749-6696; www.pearlsrainbow.com.

Bedding (Not So Gay)

Duval House (815 Duval St.) is one of the nicest mainstream guesthouses in town (with the paradoxical benefit of being right on the gay block). Expect a colonial-style house with a Tahitian garden and pool. Rates: $185–$350; Ph. 800-223-8825; www.duvalhousekeywest .com.

The award-winning Marquesa Hotel (600 Fleming St.) is top of the line. Rates: $175–$430; Ph. 800-869-4631 or 305-292-1919; www.marquesa.com.

Heron House (512 Simonton St.). Old-fashioned charm makes this an excellent choice. Rates: $159–$389; 888-861-9066; www.heronhouse.com.

Q FACT

Tennessee Williams wrote *The Night of the Iguana* and *The Rose Tattoo* while living in Key West.

Bar Tab

Key West's gay scene is limited to about two blocks along Duval. Aqua (711 Duval St.) has a daily happy hour, drag shows, and dancing. KWest Men (711 Duval St.) features strippers who bare all. La Te Da's Crystal Room Cabaret (1125 Duval St.) also offers drag shows. 801 (801 Duval St.) is a bar with live entertainment. The One Saloon (801 Duval St.) is Key West's leather/Levi's bar. Bourbon Street Pub (724 Duval St.) is another popular bar with male strippers. Bootleggers (411 Petronia St.) is a country and western dance bar. The Atlantic Shores Resort holds a popular Sunday tea dance. And Pearl's Patio is Key West's principal lesbian bar.

In and Out

Key West is the last island in a chain of islands extending south of mainland Florida. Key West is 160 miles

Q FACT

In Lawrence Grobel's *Conversations with Capote*, Truman Capote recounts that he was once in a Key West bar when a woman asked him to autograph her navel with an eyebrow pencil. With a sigh, Capote obliged. The woman's husband, peeved, came over to Capote, unzipped his fly and angrily asked if the author would like to sign his body part too. Capote allegedly glanced down at the man's penis and responded, "Well, I'm not sure, but perhaps I could initial it."

A KEY WEST DAY

Breakfast at your guesthouse, or if you feel like getting out for a bit, head to Croissants de France (816 Duval St).

Take a walk through Ripley's Believe It or Not Museum (108 Duval St.), which has 13 galleries, including a Hemingway gallery, where you can see his reading glasses and typewriter. It's cheesy, but fun.

Stroll along the gay section of Duval Street, between Angela and Olivia Streets. Skip lunch and have a slice of key lime pie from the Key Lime Pie Factory (802 Duval Street). Go crazy and get a frozen Key Lime Pie on a Stick (dipped in chocolate), too.

Buy a cool gift at Cocktail Party (808 Duval St.). They have plenty of funky stemware you won't find at Crate and Barrel. And they don't even have a Web site, so you can't get their products without a trip to Key West.

Have a poolside cocktail at the Bourbon Street Pub (New Orleans Guesthouse). The pub starts serving at 11 a.m. and doesn't stop till 4 a.m.

Catch sunset at Mallory Square.

Enjoy dinner on the patio of Bagatelle (115 Duval St.). The house, built by a sea captain, was erected in 1884. End your meal with a café con leche and smoke a hand-rolled cigar (they sell flavored ones across the street—chocolate, cherry, and vanilla.)

Catch a show at La Te Da's Crystal Room Cabaret (1125 Duval St.). Yes it's drag, but it's well worth it.

QUOTE

"In a relatively short period, Key West has become one of the most interesting communities in the country, mainly because of a kind of de facto social experiment that's going on. The basic Key West—a conservative, even red-neck community of families, including many military families, is in the process of becoming a mixed gay and straight town, and so far the mixture is working."

—Dennis Sanders, *Gay Source*, 1977

south of Miami. To get to Key West by car, take U.S. 1 south. Key West International Airport (EYW) is serviced by several major airlines.

Pages

David Leddick's *My Worst Date* is set in Miami and tells the story of 16-year-old Hugo, who ends up in bed with his mother's boyfriend.

Chris Cox's *A Key West Companion* is an informational guide to the island.

Jeffrey Epstein and Eddie Shapiro, *Queens in the Kingdom: The Ultimate Gay and Lesbian Guide to the Disney Theme Parks,* is useful if you're planning a trip to a theme park.

Gwen Cooper's *Diary of a South Beach Bombshell* is a roman à clef about Miami in its 1990s heyday.

Key West 2720 A.D. by William Eakins is a futuristic novel in which gays have been forced into permanent exile, but find sanctuary in Key West.

Biographies of gay playwright Tennessee Williams include Donald Spoto, *The Kindness of Strangers: The Life of Tennessee Williams* and Lyle Leverich, *Tom: The Unknown Tennessee Williams.*

CHAPTER SIX

Serenity in Saugatuck

SITUATED ON THE SHORES of Lake Michigan, the twin towns of Saugatuck and Douglas have a proudly All-American feel. They are more quilting bee than Queer Nation, but that hasn't stopped them from becoming the proud capital of gay beach life in the Midwest.

A little more than two hours from Chicago, Saugatuck prides itself on being a laid-back, "let's-go-antiquing" sort of town. But the eight square blocks of Saugatuck have plenty of sophisticated restaurants, funky boutiques, and critically acclaimed art galleries. Meanwhile, Douglas, on the other side of the Kalamazoo River, is only a mile away.

Like many gay beach resorts, Saugatuck has a re-spected history as an artists' colony. It is home to the world-renowned Ox-Bow School of Art, and numer-ous midwestern painters, sculptors, photographers, and writers have settled here. The town vibrates with a mix-ture of Algonquian, French-Canadian, and Old West influences.

You can visit Saugatuck any time of the year; bed-and-breakfasts are open straight through the winter.

Q FACT

Way back in 1946, the director of the Veteran's Center in Kent County, MI, urged the U.S. Navy to liberalize its strict stance on homosexuality.

(In addition to being the region's major gay resort town, Saugatuck prides itself on being the "bed-and-breakfast capital of the Midwest.") You may be surprised by the sheer beauty of Michigan's sandy lakeshore beach, not to mention the strength of the waves. But as a beach town, the main summer season is brief.

While Saugatuck certainly ranks as one of the nation's most popular gay beach resorts (at least among Midwesterners), sunbathing itself is only one part of the draw to this area. Saugatuck's Mason Street Warehouse theater produces classic musicals and some world-premiere plays (a recent season included a production of the gayish *Altar Boys* and homowright Nicky Silver's *The Food Chain*). Outdoorsy types do things like rent kayaks—Running Rivers offers guided tours, instruction, and rentals—and climb the 282 steps to the top of the area's highest sand dune, Mount Baldhead, from which you can take in impressive views of Lake Michigan. A twenty-minute drive will bring you to the Fenn Valley Winery, where you can taste dry Rieslings and a red called Capriccio.

While the Midwest is not known for its nightlife (dinner is generally served at 6 p.m. and bars close by midnight), Douglas boasts the Dunes Resort, an all-in-one disco, cocktail lounge, and video bar. There's also a game room, a fenced-in sundeck, and a swimming pool (no nudity allowed), not to mention the occasional piano cabaret show. The Dunes, which claims to be the largest gay resort in the Midwest, occupies a 20-acre property and is usually gay visitors' first choice in lodging.

Wherever you stay in the Saugatuck-Douglas area (and there isn't much difference between the two towns), you'll need to rent a car. Nothing is really within walking distance.

Sand

Saugatuck's Oval Beach has been rated one of the twenty-five best shorelines in the world by Condé Nast. From Saugatuck, take Lake Street to the Blue Star Highway, turn right on St. Peters and then left on Westshore, right on Ferry, and left on Perryman. At the sand, take a right (heading north) to the gay area. Be careful: the surf is very strong.

Calories

Toulouse (248 Culver St., Saugatuck; 616-857-1561) is considered one of the top restaurants in the region. Despite the traditional décor, the food can be somewhat

Q FACT

In the 1980s, the Michigan Womyn's Festival was plagued with conflict over whether or not to admit the male children of female festival-goers.

GAY EVE

Once upon a time, in a land, far, far away, Gay Pride was a meaningful and magical holiday. Thousands marched in the streets to demand gay liberation and protest the oppressiveness of the past.

Gay Pride has become a global phenomenon, with parades in almost every country of the non-Muslim world. But something has gotten lost over the years. Blame it on the cultural normalization of gay life, the death of the 1970s militant spirit, the yearly bickering over the best way to present our community's public image, collective frustration over our lack of inspiring leaders, or a genetic tendency toward cynicism—Gay Pride has become as soulless and superficial as a circuit party.

In 2002, after seeing the New York City production of *Last Sunday in June*, a group of friends and I organized the first Gay Eve, the Saturday night before Pride. Using the Passover Seder as a model, we had a dinner party in the West Village with the explicit aim of "celebrating the privileges and acknowledging the challenges" of being gay.

On that first Gay Eve, we passed around 3"×5" cards with names of gay personages from history. Since our group ranged in age from early twenties to late fifties, every name evoked a different response. Some were shocked to learn that so-and-so was gay, others grew reminiscent when certain names from recent decades were read. After dinner, we shared stories of growing up gay.

I have now celebrated Gay Eve in various locales, including a restaurant in the Hamptons and with housemates on Fire Island. Since Pride always falls on a summer weekend, I think a gay beach home is the perfect place to hold Gay Eve. All you need are some companions, a few bottles of wine or pink champagne, good food (I like to make things that are symbolic of being gay—Greek salad seems very apropos) and some questions to start the conversation. "What do you like most about being gay?" "What would you like most to tell your parents that you've never told them?" "If you had the chance, would you ever choose to be straight?" The more provocative the question, the better the conversation is likely to be.

After dinner, you could watch a gay classic, like *Making Love* or *The Boys in the Band*. Or you could share letters to long-lost loves.

However you choose to celebrate Gay Eve, I think you end up remembering the evening for many years afterwards, if not the rest of your life. Everyone needs a time for a little spiritual reflection, and the evening before Pride seems like the perfect time for us.

nouvelle. The Café Sir Douglas (333 Blue Star Hwy., Douglas; 616-857-1401) is located in the Dunes. People eat here because it's convenient and gay-popular, not for the food. Pumpernickel's Eatery (202 Butler St., Saugatuck) is the place to go for breakfast in Saugatuck. Be sure to have their signature cinnamon rolls.

Bedding

The Dunes Resort (333 Blue Star Hwy., Douglas). Eighty-one rooms and an ongoing pool party all summer long make this the most popular gay resort in the area. Even if you choose to stay somewhere else (or can't get a room), you'll end up coming to the Dunes for your evening activities. The Dunes even has three women's weekends off-season each year. Rates: $65–$185; Ph.: 269-857-1401; www.dunesresort.com.

The Kirby House Bed and Breakfast (294 West Center St., Saugatuck). Boasting stained-glass windows, Oriental rugs, and five fireplaces, the Kirby House is a true Victorian cottage. But a heated pool, Jacuzzi and free wireless Internet add nice modern comforts. Gay-owned. Rates: $115–$185; Ph.: 800-521-6473; www.kirbyhouse.com.

The Newnham Suncatcher Inn (131 Griffith St., Saugatuck). A little more on the kitschy side (think stuffed animals and knickknacks), rooms named Holly Hobbie and Victoria Secret. Owned by a lesbian couple. Rates: $105–$135; Ph.: 800-587-4249; suncatcherinn.com.

Beachwood Manor Inn (736 Pleasant St., Saugatuck). An 1870s Greek Revival house with three guestrooms, each with private bath. All rooms have cable TV, DVD players, fireplaces, and wireless Internet.

Rates: $150–$300; Ph.: 877-857-1587; www.beech woodmanorinn.com.

The Belvedere Inn (3656 63rd St.). Located three miles outside of town, the Belvedere is an upscale inn with its own formal restaurant and five acres of grounds for strolling. Perfect for a commitment ceremony in grand, Gatsby fashion. (Note: the Belvedere is not a gay-owned property.). Ph.: 269-857-5777; www.thebel vedereinn.com. Call for rates.

In and Out

Saugatuck and Douglas are located 40 miles southwest of Grand Rapids, so your best bet for a visit to these beach towns is to fly into Grand Rapids' Gerald R. Ford International Airport, rent a car, and go. For those from the coasts, rental car rates will seem especially cheap in this part of the country. Driving from Chicago along the coast (via I-94 east and I-196 N) will take you two hours, and driving from Detroit (via I-96 west) will take you three.

Hotel Rates

When booking your hotel, don't forget to check Web sites like hotels.com and orbitz.com. Even some "gay-only" hotels show up on these sites. While you may not actually get the cheapest price (it's always a good idea to visit the hotel's own Web site), these sites are particularly convenient when traveling to countries where you don't speak the language.

L.A.'s gay beach is in the heart of Malibu.

CHAPTER SEVEN

The Little Beaches

ASIDE FROM THE "BIG FOUR," there are baby beaches throughout the U.S. Anywhere there's sun and surf, you are likely to find a patch of sand that's been claimed by gay men. I can't cover all the gay beaches in the country, but below are some favorites worth visiting if you're looking for something new or happen to be in the area.

Sandy Hook, NJ

(one and a half hours from NYC)

Who was it who so cleverly determined that Beach G (for Gunniston) should be reserved for the gays? In reality, it's also for straight nudists, but it happens to be Sandy Hook's only gay beach, and a very nice one.

To get to Sandy Hook by car, take the Holland Tunnel to the NJ Turnpike South. At Exit 11 take the Garden State Parkway to Exit 117 and follow Route 36 East toward Gateway National Recreation Area. Once you get to Route 36 there will be plenty of signs to Sandy Hook. There's a parking fee of $10 a day (season passes cost $60). You can also take a ferry from lower Manhattan. The ferry departs from South Street Seaport, Pier 16, every day at 9:20 a.m., 11:20 a.m., and 1:30 p.m. Walk-up round-trip ferry ticket price is $32 Adult/$22 Child (there is a slight discount for tickets purchased in advance). Web: www.circleline-downtown.com. Look for Beach G.

Sandy Hook has only 5,000 parking spaces, and during busy summer weekends those spaces fill up fast. Many a time I have made the one-and-a-half hour drive, only to be turned away at the gate. On a Saturday or Sunday, plan to arrive before 10 a.m. (at the latest) or after 3 p.m.

There's a fast food stand at the entrance to the beach, as well as showers and bathrooms.

Asbury Park, NJ
(two hours from NYC)

Isn't there something inherently gay about the idea of finding a piece of property in a run-down neighborhood, turning it into a beautiful home, then sitting back and watching as the surrounding real estate quadruples in value? Back in the 1990s, when Asbury Park was still one of New Jersey's most dangerous neighborhoods, only the gays had the vision to purchase and renovate the Victorian mansions that line Asbury Avenue. After all, most of them had become crack dens. Even now, between all the rainbow-flag-flying, gorgeously redone summer homes, stand a few recalcitrant heroin houses. But if you could once find a mind-boggling bargain in Asbury Park, now you'll have to settle for a decent deal.

What makes Asbury Park so appealing despite the persistence of winter gangs and pickpockets on the beach is its proximity to Manhattan and the determined spirit of a few key developers to restore the town's former luster. Before the 1970s, Asbury Park was as charming as any of its seaside neighbors, with a famed boardwalk. In fact, it was known as the "Jewel of the Jersey Shore." But white flight in the seventies changed the town's demographics and led to an influx of drugs and crime. In the early 2000s, upper-middle-class gays began to reclaim the town, which, after all, offers prime sunbathing right on the Atlantic Ocean.

To get to Asbury Park from Manhattan, take the NJ Turnpike South to Exit 11, and then take the Garden State Parkway South to Exit 102, Asbury Park. Bear right off the exit ramp onto Asbury Avenue and continue heading east all the way to the ocean, following the signs to Asbury Park.

A one-day beach pass is $5. A season pass is $45. Passes can be purchased on the boardwalk at 3rd and Ocean Avenue.

If you fall in love while you're in Asbury Park and want to get hitched, Civil Union Applications are available at City Hall. The processing cost is $28 and can be paid by check or money order. Civil union applications are also available for downloading at www. state.nj.us/health/vital/forms.shtml.

East Hampton, NY
(three to six hours from Manhattan, depending on traffic)

The Hamptons are essentially a sandy version of the Upper East Side (only with more traffic and fewer trees). If you simply can't resist the opportunity to see what makes the Hamptons so extraordinarily popular with New York City's rich, then you too can ride the Jitney, made famous outside New York by *Sex and the City*. The Hampton Jitney (a bus for those would normally

"The Hampton's Jitney is just like the bus to summer camp. Only instead of singing songs, everyone ignores each other and talks on their cell phones."

—Carrie on *Sex and the City*

never dream of taking public transportation) departs regularly at 86th Street (between 3rd & Lexington on the north side of 86th), at 69th Street (west side of Lexington between 69th & 68th in front of the Hunter College Art Gallery), at 59th Street (west side of Lexington between 59th & 60th across from Bloomingdales), and at 40th Street (between 3rd & Lexington on the south side of 40th). For more information, go to www.hamptonjitney.com.

East Hampton is the gayest of the group and you'll find the Gucci-wearing boys at Two Mile Hollow Beach. Jerry Seinfeld and art dealer Larry Gagosian live nearby. Be careful before you decide to engage in any illicit activity: a scandal erupted in 2003 when men were arrested in the Two Mile Hollow beach parking lot for inappropriate and unlawful behavior. (An *East Hampton Star* editorial called the arrests a "witch hunt").

Surprisingly, there are no gay bars left in the Hamptons anymore. Then again, there aren't many bars on the Upper East Side either.

Jacob Riis Park, NY
(One to one and a half hours from Manhattan)
Much closer to Manhattan than East Hampton, Jacob Riis Park features a nice sand beach and an early 20th century bathhouse listed on the National Register of Historic Places (no, not that kind of bathhouse). The park was originally designed as a destination for New York City's well-to-do, but they have since moved on to other locales. The nice thing about Jacob Riis Park is that it is (almost) accessible by subway. To get there,

CHRISTOPHER STREET PIER (MANHATTAN)

Those of us who do not have summer shares will often head down to the Christopher Street Pier for an afternoon of sunbathing on the grass. Granted, there's no high tea, but you can get one of many flavors of iced tea at the convenient food stand. They also sell fruit and cheese plates, sandwiches, and assorted snacks. Take the 1 or 9 train to Christopher Street and head west.

take the 2 train to Flatbush Ave., and then the Q35 bus to Riis Beach. From Manhattan, the entire journey will take you an hour. Admission to the beach is free. Head to the east end.

Laguna Beach, CA
(one to two hours from Los Angeles, depending on traffic)
If there's one thing you'll notice about Laguna, it's that even the city workers sweeping the streets have the golden blond locks and sparkling blue eyes of movie stars. Maybe no place evokes the classic image of Southern California like Laguna Beach. San Diego is great for dog owners and nature lovers. LA is perfect for power lunches. But Laguna Beach is where you go if you want 1960s-style Beach Blanket Bingo (or Babylon).

The irony is that Laguna Beach is prime Orange County real estate, Orange being one of the most conservative counties in the country. But Laguna was once an artists' colony, and "artists" has almost always equaled "gay." At Laguna, you'll see aspiring models mixed in with Orange County families who still believe homosexual teachers don't belong in schools.

Getting to Laguna is the easy part—just drive south on the Pacific Coast Highway. (It's 60 miles from L.A.) Getting to West Street Beach, the main gay area, is a little more challenging. It's a steep slope down to the sand, but there are several sets of paved steps (99 steps to be exact) for your sunbathing convenience (one set is on the south side of the condo complex at 31423 South Coast Highway. There's another set at 31351 South Coast Highway).

As of this writing, the one gay bar in Laguna is set to close, so it's possible the area's gay appeal will fade.

Will Rogers State Beach, Pacific Palisades, CA

(twenty minutes from West Hollywood)

Ask an L.A. gay where the nearest gay beach is, and he's likely to look at you with confusion. Despite its reputation for sun and surf, Los Angeles is not a beach town. L.A. guys prefer to do their sunning poolside. Private pools are more exclusive, they cost a fortune to maintain, and it's easier to negotiate with your agent on your cell phone in a lounge chair than on a towel. The most popular gay "beach" resort for L.A. gays, Palm Springs, has no beach at all. It's a collection of hotels with pools.

But in a pinch, Angelinos will head to Will Rogers Beach in Pacific Palisades (or "Ginger Rogers," as it is often called). In fact, gays without pools have been coming here since the 1940s, when there was a gay bar nearby. It's a public beach, with a parking lot that charges only $8 for the whole day. Free parking can sometimes be had on the other side of Pacific Highway; if you find it, there's a convenient underground pass leading to the beach. From West Hollywood, take the 405 to the 10 and then head to the right (north) at Pacific Coast Highway. Will Rogers Beach stretches for several miles, but the gay section is only at the intersection of Pacific Coast Highway and Entrada. There's a food stand at the beach, billing itself as "Little Mykonos," which sells excellent burgers. The sand is gritty and not the cleanest. The surf is strong.

Black's Beach, La Jolla, CA
(thirty minutes from San Diego)

Anyone who's ever been to Black's Beach is likely to be very proud of that fact. Of all the gay beaches in the U.S., it is surely the hardest to get to. And even harder to get from. Black's Beach is situated at the base of a very high mountain cliff in La Jolla, California. By the time you reach the bottom, you will wonder how you are ever going to get back up to the top. Then again, while I was steadily making my way down, some San Diego native with his pair of black labs bounded up the trail in the opposite direction, making me look like the true, nature-dreading city-boy that I am.

The only reason that I elected to brave the journey to Black's Beach is its most famous erstwhile resident: Jefferson Poland, founder, in 1964, of the Sexual Freedom League, an organization that helped in its own small way to usher in the hippie era and the gay liberation movement. After Poland had a falling-out with fellow League members in the 1970s (his fellow leaguers were straights who didn't like Poland's avowed bisexuality), he settled on Black's Beach and made it the capital of a new movement to promote nudism. To this day, Black's Beach remains proudly naturist.

If you're really feeling adventuresome, try paragliding. The Torrey Pines Gliderport, on the cliffs above Black's Beach, offers "in tandem" lessons for $150. After you step off the edge of the cliff, you will soar over the beach, the water, and the backyard swimming pools of nearby estates. I still can't quite believe that I actually did it. Only about four people die paragliding in the country each year. (Seriously.)

Ogunquit, ME
(one and a half hours from Boston)

Maine may seem like an unusual state to house a gay beach (or a beach of any sort) but in fact it is home to one of the nicest (and most up-and-coming) gay beaches. Ogunquit (Native American for "beautiful place by the sea") offers three miles of practically pristine sand. And while Maine may indeed be grim during the winter, in summertime it is one of the most beautiful states in the union. Mainers aren't known for being warm or welcoming (this is Stephen King land), but they are exceptionally tolerant and liberal-minded. For many years now, Portland, Maine, has had a large lesbian community.

You don't go to Maine for chic clubs or late-night dancing (there are only two bars in town—Maine Street and Five-O's) but for the classic New England experience, which includes antiquing, lobster-eating, and reading Thoreau (or, alternatively, searching for bargains at Maine's multitude of outlets). If you're the nature-loving type, you might also want to do all those nature-oriented activities that people claim to enjoy like hiking and birdwatching.

To get to Ogunquit from Boston, take 95 North till you hit the exit for York, and then continue North on Route 1. Ogunquit is about a half-hour south of Portland.

Rock River, VT
(three hours from Boston; four and a half hours from NYC)

There's something especially fitting about sunbathing nude in Vermont. The state has always been a rebel outpost, ever since the Green Mountain Boys proclaimed the Independent Republic of Vermont in the late 1700s (Vermont was NOT one of the original thirteen colonies). Besides, Vermont was originally settled by French explorers, who it's hard to imagine were not more liberal-minded about love and sex than their English colonial neighbors in Massachusetts and New Hampshire. Perhaps not surprisingly given its history. Vermont was the first state in the nation to grant legal recognition to civil unions for gay couples.

Getting to the nude section of the Rock River Beach is not for the timid. After parking your car, you walk along the south riverbank for about twenty minutes. (That alone can be treacherous in spots). When you're almost at the beach you must cross the river. The water can reach up to your rib cage and the current is swift. If you survive the river crossing, you head upstream and you'll see men plopped down here and there. On a good weekend day there are about fifty to seventy-five men, generally 35 or older (okay, it can't be that dangerous). The river is full of big boulders and you can sit on a rock right in the water. It's very laid-back. Needless to say, you must bring all food and drink with you as there is nothing available for purchase.

If you intend to stay in the area, check out A Stone Wall Inn (802-875-4238; www.astonewallinn.com), which is equal parts gay guesthouse and pioneer in environmental design. (Children are not permitted as guests.) From New York or Massachusetts, take I-91 to Exit 6 at Rockingham to Rt.103 North to Chester. Continue straight through the town, picking up Rt.11 towards Londonderry. Turn left on Rt. 121 and go to the first four-way intersection. Take a left on Hitchcock Hill Road. At about seven-tenths of a mile, turn right at the sign. Hotel owners Bob and Steven can direct you to the river.

Hippie Hollow, TX
(one and a half hours from Austin)
Hmmm, sunbathing naked on a gay beach in Texas. Doesn't sound to everyone like the brightest idea in the

world. Hippie Hollow is great—as long as you don't mind the rocks and stay clear of the cops. To many, the idea of time spent in a Texas jailhouse just for being queer is an experience they'd rather miss. But if you're curious, or like to live on the edge, from Austin take I-35 North or Rt. 1 North to Highway 2222 West to RR 620 South. Take RR 620 South 1.3 miles to Comanche Trail. Turn right on Comanche Trail and travel 2 miles. Park entrance is on your left. There's an $8 a day permit fee. The beach gets as busy as a bar selling dollar drinks (especially on Splash Day, held annually in late spring). Bring a quarter for your telephone call and the number of a good, New York City lawyer.

Russian River, CA

(one and a half hours from San Francisco)

Yes, once upon a time this heavily forested area was known as "Big Bottom." Now it's simply known as the getaway for boho San Franciscans (that's short for "bohemian homosexuals," in case you're not in the know), big ol' bears, and their admirers. There are over thirty gay and gay-friendly resorts and inns along the river's shores. Visitors pour in for both Lazy Bear Week and Women's Week.

Russian River is actually a string of communities. Some of the most popular include Guerneville, Monte Rio, Forestville, Rio Nido, Duncans Mills, and Occidental. Guerneville actually has the second-highest concentration of same-sex households in the U.S.

The great advantage of Russian River is its year-round perfect weather, with an average temperature in the low 80s and sunshine 90% of the time. You've also got all those redwoods, which provide ample shade. This is nature-lover's territory, with excellent canoeing, kayaking, hiking, bicycling, and the like. You can also indulge in hot-air ballooning or visit some of the 250 wineries for which Sonoma County is so famous.

To get to Guerneville from San Francisco, drive north on Highway 101 to Highway 116 West and exit at Cotati. Turn left onto Highway 116 West and drive through Sebastopol and Forestville toward Jenner. Turn left on River Road once you cross over the Russian River.

Nude sunbathing is popular near the Wohler Bridge riverbank. Look for the green gate just before the bridge. It leads to the twenty-minute trail to the beach (the trail will start on your right, just after you pass through the gate).

Bedding in Russian River

Highlands Resort (1400 Woodland Dr., Guerneville). Features a clothing-optional pool, outdoor hot tub, and a rustic feel. $60–$190; Ph.: 707-869-0333; www.High landsResort.com.

Russian River Resort (16390 Fourth St., Guernev-ille). A little more modern than the Highlands, with newly designed rooms, and in the heart of downtown Guerneville. The pool gets pretty crowded in summer. $65–$200; Ph.: 707-869-0691; www.RussianRiverRe sort.com.

Sonoma Orchid Inn (12850 River Rd., Guerneville). The Sonoma Orchid bills itself as "a country-elegant, cozy and comfortable bed and breakfast." This is less "bear country," and more wine taster's land. The rooms have names like Sequoia, Hawthorne, and Madrone. Rates: $140–$245; Ph.: 888-877-4466; www.sonomaorchidinn .com.

Galveston, TX

(forty-five minutes to one hour from Houston)

People like to say that Galveston Island isn't really part of Texas, and it certainly feels different from the rest of the Lone Star State. This 32-mile-long island (only 2½ miles wide) exudes both Southern charm and European luxury. On Galveston you will be able to visit such pre-modern mansions as the Ashton Villa (1859), the Bishop's Palace (1886), and the Moody Mansion (1895). The

FOR THOSE WITH A MILITARY FETISH . . .

Colonel Bubbie's sells surplus uniforms and accessories from the Civil War, Spanish American War, WWI, WWII, Korean War, Vietnam, and Desert Storm, not to mention current-issue military garb. They have a giant warehouse filled to the brim with all your military needs. Open Monday through Friday 9 a.m.–4 p.m., Saturday 9 a.m.–5 p.m. Closed Sunday. 2202 Strand Ave., Galveston, TX 77550; Ph.: 800-231-6005; www .colbubbie.com.

Grand 1894 Opera House is ranked among the nation's finest historical theaters.

The most popular parts of the island—the Strand and the Harborside—are walk-able (another thing that sets this resort apart from the rest of its home state). But there's also a replica streetcar if you're feeling nostalgic.

Part of Galveston's LGBT history is the story of colorful Miss Bettie Brown, a Galveston native, who once occupied the Ashton Villa. The daughter of one of the island's richest businessmen, Miss Bettie nevertheless broke all the rules. She drank, smoked, and had a close female companion whom she was never seen without. According to legend, she had two sets of horses: black ones for daytime riding and white ones for evening. Miss Bettie remained unmarried to her dying day, and rumors circulated about her "bohemian" lifestyle. Ashton Villa is said to be haunted by her carefree and wild ghost.

Galveston's best gay bar (situated right on the main gay beach) is the Blvd. Saloon, which features glass walls facing the ocean, and a two-level oceanfront deck.

To get to Galveston from Houston, take I-45 South. Once you hit the Island it becomes Broadway Street.

CHAPTER EIGHT

The Magic of Mykonos

QUOTE

The isles of Greece, the Isles of Greece!
Where burning Sappho loved and sung,
Where grew the arts of war and peace,
Where Delos rose, and Phoebus sprung!
Eternal summer gilds them yet,
But all, except their sun, is set.

—Lord Byron, *Don Juan*

THE JEWS have Jerusalem, the Muslims have Mecca, the Catholics have Rome, and the gays, well, the gays will always have Mykonos. While San Francisco may be the political capital of queerdom, Mykonos is the gay spiritual homeland. A visit to Mykonos—and the nearby isle of Delos—is a return to one's gayest roots. Whether you're Greek passive or Greek active (or too young to remember what those terms actually mean), you will find a new sense of belonging on this blue and white atoll in the middle of the Aegean, 95 miles east of Athens. For thousands of years, gay men have been making a summertime pilgrimage to this sunwashed land. On Mykonos, you will rediscover the polymorphously perverse world that reigned in the era of Achilles and Agamemnon. Greece has over a thousand islands, but only one of them is a gay landmark.

The first time I visited Mykonos, I was a college student on summer break. For some reason, places like Provincetown and Fire Island seemed intimidating. Going to them meant you were "officially" gay. Mykonos was something else: distant, exotic, historically significant, mythological, adventurous. I'd long wanted to go to Greece to experience firsthand the birthplace of Western culture. When I learned there was an island especially welcoming to gay men, I knew I had to go.

Mykonos is situated in the Aegean; it is part of the Cycladic group of islands, famous for their white-washed houses that stand in sharp contrast to the sparkling blue sea. You've probably seen countless pictures of Mykonos's cobblestone streets and trademark windmills without realizing you were looking at images of a gay getaway. What those images don't usually show are the vast number of gay men who flock to the island every summer from around the world.

The residents of this magical island say it gets its unique atmosphere from the wind that sweeps off of Delos, the tiny island at the center of the Cycladic chain. (More about Delos later). That wind, known as the "Meltemi," is actually quite strong, so it keeps Mykonos pleasantly cool even on the sunniest of days. Whatever the source of the island's atmosphere, a unique atmosphere it is. Mykonos is equally welcoming to straights and gays alike. This isn't Fire Island or the Castro. This isn't a gay ghetto where we've managed to set up a safe enclave apart from the rest of the world. This is a social baklava, where gays and straights swirl together, like so many nuts and raisins in a sweet embrace.

The main town, known as Chora, sits on the bay. (You will see backpackers sleeping on the harbor beach, but don't be confused—this isn't the sand for sunbathing.) The town of Mykonos was built on a hill up from the harbor. Its narrow winding streets were designed to keep out invaders. They also manage to baffle tourists. Throw away your compass and just wander (cars are prohibited). Take every little side street and alleyway—you never know what secret you'll discover.

While Mykonos is famous for its beaches named Paradise and Super Paradise, don't expect a lush, tropical island. According to legend, Mykonos was formed when Hercules, in one of his twelve tasks, killed the Giants and threw them into the sea; they petrified and turned into huge rocks, forming what is now homo heaven. As the tale suggests, Mykonos is extremely arid and almost entirely lacking in vegetation. It's also the smallest of the Cyclades. But don't let such geographic details fool you. For one thing, Mykonos is beautiful, in the way any gay destination ought to be. It is indeed covered in those traditional whitewashed houses you've seen in photos, each with bright blue shutters that match the azure hue of the Aegean. Old-fashioned windmills (not those funky, postmodern things you see on the drive from L.A. out to Palm Springs), dot the island, capturing the life force of the Meltemi. And while the island may be small, the party culture is nonstop. Whether you're sunbathing on the beach or dancing up a storm at a nightclub, music with a good beat will never be far away. All the major beaches sport cafés and cute bars. And Chora is home to dozens of clubs.

Mykonos got its name from Mykons, the grandson of Apollo, god of music, male beauty, and bisexuality. While most of the beaches of Mykonos offer nude sunbathing (including some of the family beaches), *our* beach is known as Super Paradise. It's rocky (which is a good thing, given the strong breeze of the Meltemi, since sand would blow into your eyes) and secluded. Those with cars or mopeds can get there directly, but I like the traditional adventure of taking a bus from Chora, followed by a miniboat taxi ride to the beach. Nudity and swimsuits mix on Super Paradise; what you won't find are a lot of women.

If you're feeling restless, you can spend a day at—not exclusively homo but definitely gay-friendly—Paradise, a beach that also has water sports and a diving center.

Mykonos may be Greece, but Greek food can be surprisingly hard to find. Most of the restaurants are

Italian or "continental." The day follows a standard schedule: sleep in till 10, have a quick breakfast in town, hit the beach, have lunch at an outdoor café, enjoy a cocktail at one of the sunset bars in the area known as Little Venice, take a nap, eat dinner at 10, go clubbing till 3 or 4, and then start all over again.

The sunset bars are one of the true highlights of a Mykonos vacation. Around six, those in the know make a mad rush to the bars facing the horizon. Then everyone acts perfectly calm. You'll enjoy the sea gently lapping at the reef as you sip your drink and listen to the latest tunes. Remember to bring something stylish with you to the beach to wear at sunset so you don't feel like a tacky tourist.

Speaking of style, Mykonos is the Aegean capital of leather. (No, not that kind of leather). The cobblestone streets of Chora smell delightfully pungent from the vast array of leather goods shops. Make sure you leave room in your luggage for a few expensive trinkets. Be forewarned: the streets of Mykonos town are a maze. Literally. According to legend, the town was built in such a way that Phoenician raiders would get befuddled before they managed to find the real loot.

After a few days on Mykonos, it will be time to do some sightseeing. That's when you'll make the trek to Delos. Ferries depart every morning and you can buy a ticket at any tourist office in town. Delos is tiny, so you'll readily spot its most unusual landmark: a pair of twin monuments to masculinity. Yes, the ancient Greeks erected giant phalli in honor of the male principle. And when I say "giant," I mean *giant*. Forget those ten inches you see advertised on Web sites. We're talking twenty-foot-tall, hard-as-rock (literally) penises pointed directly at the sky. Each one has smooth balls the size of boulders. Lest there be any confusion, these phallic structures aren't metaphorical symbols à la the Hindu lingam. These are literal representations of the male anatomy. Alas, weather and war have decapitated both, so we'll never know what they looked like in their full, unsheathed glory. But don't let that deter you. A mere moment in the presence of these pillars of penile veneration will forever change your perspective on the history of sex.

Delos is what originally made this region of the world our cultural and emotional epicenter. The legendary birthplace of Apollo, god of male beauty, and his twin sister, Artemis (who once killed a man simply because he saw her nude), Delos eventually evolved into the financial capital of the Athenian empire.

While you're on Delos, take a look at the image carved into the base of one of the twin phalli. The ancient Greeks apparently had just as much of a sense of bawdy humor as we do. The image is a carved picture of a rooster. As in English, the Greek slang word for rooster has sexual connotations.

Mykonos had its heyday in the 1970s, when debauchery was glamorous and every famous person in the world was bisexual. In those days, models and rock stars mingled among hippies, all of whom appreciated the island's anything-goes atmosphere. Things slowed down in the eighties and nineties, but the Mykonot spirit lives on. With Greece's entry into the E.U., prices have skyrocketed, so it now has a more refined ambience. Still, if you don't mind a lot of guys taking off

Q FACT

their Prada swimsuits when they get to the beach, book your trip to Mykonos ASAP.

Sand

Getting to the beach is part of the Mykonos adventure. It starts with bus, taxi or moped to Plati Yialos (pronounced "Plati galos"). To take the bus, you follow the crowds to the south bus station (it's not really a station, just an outdoor stop). Tell someone you want to get to the beach. (The bus is cheap and fun.) A taxi to Plati Yialos will set you back some (and could take longer as you will have to wait on line at the taxi stand); a moped is great if you're not afraid of killing yourself on the island's sharp rocky cliffs. From Plati Yialos, you will take a waterbus (or "caique") to one of "our" beaches. Paradise is a nude, mostly mixed beach. Super Paradise is the main gay destination. Both have cafés and dance music, which make you feel a little like you're on a gay cruise ship.

If you get bored with Paradise or Super Paradise, Mykonos has dozens of other beaches. Explore on foot and you never know when you'll find your own private cove. Other gay-friendly beaches on the Island include Elia and Agios Sostis.

DELOS

Delos was the birthplace of Apollo and Artemis, the twin gods of gayness and lesbianism. Apollo was the gorgeous music player, god of sunlight and sex and male beauty. His sister, Artemis, was the serious one. A huntress with a lithe, boyish body, she was a sworn virgin for life. In fact, she once killed a man who happened to see her naked by having him ripped to shreds by a horde of bucks.

Over time, the social significance of Delos evolved. At one point it became a place to worship Dionysus, god of theatre and wine (and arguably just as queer as Apollo). In fact, a part of the island is named the Theatre District, where you will find the House of Dionysus and the House of Masks.

To get to Delos, take a ferry from the main port in Mykonos. The trip takes 45 minutes and costs $20 round-trip. Most leave early in the morning (8:30 or 9:00 a.m.) and return in the early afternoon. (There are no hotels on Delos.) Some ferry operators include a guided tour of the island for an additional fee. Entrance is $8. Because Delos gets very strong sunshine, it's important to bring sunglasses and sunblock. The island is rocky, so wear comfortable shoes. Since food is scarce (and expensive), you might want to bring along snacks.

Calories

Mykonos is awash with restaurants; most of the better ones are Italian or "continental." Addresses on Mykonos are virtually useless; just ask at your hotel for directions. Edem, in the harbor, is a Mykonot standby with good food and a fun crowd.

Philippi, adjacent to the Hotel Philippi, is a romantic spot for a special evening. Katrin's is one of the most famous and oldest restaurants on the island, with classic French and Greek cuisine and excellent service. Caprice is in the Little Venice area, next to the bar of the same name, with tables right on the water. It serves good traditional dishes.

Mamacas, offering traditional Greek cuisine, is situated in a beautiful garden near the main square. Sale Pepe serves excellent Italian food.

Bar Tab

After a day at the beach, almost everyone heads to a select group of bars from which you can watch the sun set over the Aegean. The sunset bars are located in a neighborhood known as Little Venice. The gayest of this group of bars are Kastro, Porta and Le Caprice.

For gay men on Mykonos, the evening always begins in earnest at Pierro's, a tiny club that rules over the night. Start with a drink outside, then head indoors for some old-fashioned table dancing (think Gypsy Kings and Madonna—no circuit music here). When you need a break, head next door to Icaros, a more mellow bar that often has drag shows.

Bedding

There are two islands of Mykonos. One exists from July–August when the island gets close to a million visitors, the other in May, June, and September. They are two completely different destinations. If you're planning on visiting in July or August, you'll need to book your rooms three to six months in advance.

On the high end, Cavo Tagoo overlooks the town and has its own (saltwater) pool. Rates: $300–$600; Ph.: 22890-23-692; www.cavotagoo.com.

The Belvedere will give you the feeling of being at a traditional resort. Rates: $300–$500; Ph.: 22890-25-122; www.belvedere.com.

If you want to stay near the beach (far away from town and all its nightlife), the Kivotos Club Hotel at

MYKONOS OFF-SEASON

Mykonos is a summer destination: the sea is too cold for swimming from October to March. The island is inhabited all year long, but if you come in winter, be prepared for cold, wind, and rain.

Locals will tell you the best months to visit the island are May and September, which are considered off-season. Everything is cheaper off-season, and while less exciting for the single traveler, far more romantic for the happy couple. By far the two busiest months are July and August, when finding a room on the island can be a true challenge.

THE CYCLADES

Mykonos is one of several islands that encircle Delos—together they are known as the "encirclers," or Cyclades (pronounced "ky-klad-ays" in Greek). Every one of the Cyclades has become a popular tourist destination, though the only two that are truly on the gay map are Mykonos and Santorini. I made the mistake once of venturing off by myself to Sifnos, one of the lesser-known islands. Lesser known meant fewer hotels that I could afford, and a Catholic community that did not appreciate my nude sunbathing. Literally. Word got around the island that some obnoxious American tourist had skinny-dipped at dawn. Someone, not knowing I was the culprit, spread the gossip to me ("Can you believe what some obnoxious American tourist did yesterday morning?") and I wished I'd stayed on Mykonos.

Ornos Bay is the height of luxury. Think chilled towels for hot summer days and a pool with underwater music that's piped in. Rates: $500–$1,500; Ph.: 22890-25-795; www.kivotosclubhotel.gr.

While it's far from almost everything, I would feel deeply remiss if I didn't recommend Ortensias Villas. This is where I worked when I was 19 years old on summer vacation visiting Mykonos for the first time. I couldn't afford my own room, so the owners of the hotel gave me a job hawking rooms down at the pier. They let me eat all my meals with them and I got to know their family. Then, one day, they announced that they needed to go to Athens for the week and that I would be in charge of the hotel. They left and I "ran" the place, which mainly consisted of me going to the beach in the morning and going dancing at night and hoping there were no problems. If you stay at Ortensias Villas, please say hi to Kiki and Kostas for me. They are some of the best people on the planet. Rates: $120–$245; Ph.: 30 22890 25119; www.ortensiavillas.com.

In and Out

Mykonos can easily be reached by air from Athens (in summer months, there are more than ten flights a day). The trip takes thirty to thirty-five minutes. If you're a young buck on a tight budget, you can take a six-hour ferry. Mykonos is close to Santorini, so be sure to see the famed volcano isle of black sand.

If you happen to arrive on Mykonos without accommodations, hotel agents swarm at the ferry dock. But still, August is so popular that you may not be able to find a single free room on the island.

CHAPTER NINE

Spain: Elegant Sitges and Decadent Ibiza

A DAY IN SITGES (pronounced "sea-chez") and you may never be able to leave. Share a seafood paella lunch with new friends from around the world right on the beach, at Mare Nostrum, and you will feel as if you'd returned to Europe in the glamorous days of the early twentieth century. The palm trees of the Passeig Maritim provide a royal ambience, and the town's many mansions remind you of its wealth.

When you arrive at the train station, you will find yourself at the top of the hill on which Sitges was built. Whichever path you choose will take you down the narrow cobblestone streets of the old town, which is presided over by an eighteenth-century church. As you descend towards the water, you slowly realize you are in a beach town. When you see the bodies on the beach, you realize you are in a gay haven.

Sitges is one of the few places in the world where the gay beach is right in the heart of town. You can't miss it—it's directly in front of Restaurant Picnic. (The nude beach, Playa del Muerto, is farther away: a forty-five minute walk. Keep going past the Terramar Hotel to where the beach gets rockier. There's a second nude beach in the other direction at Playa dels Balmins. Keep going beyond the cemetery.)

Part of Sitges's claim to fame is its bright, Moderniste architecture. Led by one Santiago Rusiñol, the Modernistes flocked to Sitges in the late nineteenth century and formed their own artists' colony. Their artistic activities were helped along by a rich American patron, the scion of a prominent industrialist. Today, the Moderniste buildings give the town a unique, colorful flair. And if you're an architecture buff, you will certainly make the thirty-minute trip into Barcelona to see Gaudí's famed buildings.

Like the rest of Spain, Sitges is on a different timetable. Dinner starts at 10 p.m., drinks at midnight, and the bars don't get going till 3 a.m. You will, of course, want to visit Primer de Maig street, also known as Carrer del Picat, or the "street of sin."

Q FACT

Sitges is a year-round destination, but the water is only warm enough for swimming in summer.

No matter how early you get up or how late you sleep in, you are sure to enjoy Sitges's cobblestone streets and picturesque views.

Calories

Parrots Restaurant (18 Joan Tarrida) offers an eclectic continental mix. Ogmios (17 Bonaventura) is hip and happening. El Trull (3 Mossen Felix Clara) is intimate and satisfying. Located on the beach, Mare Nostrum (Passeig de la Ribera) is the place to go in town for paella.

The Beach House (34 Sant Pau, 93-894-90-29, reservations recommended), opened by Australian chefs Brad Downes and Michael Hutton in May 2002, has an open-air terrace and a menu that changes daily.

Q HINT

For more information on Sitges, check out www.gayin sitges.com.

Bar Tab

Sitges has two dozen gay watering holes, from sleazy to upscale. Mediterraneo (6 Bonaventura) is the big dance club, but it's also open for early cocktails (early meaning 10 p.m.). El Candil (9 Carreta) attracts a young crowd.

After the clubs close, the after-parties begin. On Tuesday nights, grab the free shuttle bus in from the Calipolis Hotel to L'Atlantida, which features outdoor dancing till dawn (check out www.gaybeachparty.com for more details). For standard circuit music (and lack of emotional effect), there's Organic (15 Bonaire) and Trailer (36 Angel Vidal).

Bedding (Gay)

Parrots Hotel and Spa (16 Calle Joan Tarrida) caters to gay men. There's free Wi-Fi in the lobby and satellite TV in every room. In town, a few minutes' walk from the beach. Ph.: 93-894-13-50. Call for rates.

Hotel Romàntic (33 Sant Isidre) and Hotel de la Renaixença (7 Isla de Cuba). A former estate converted into a hotel, the Romàntic has a charming, old-world feel. Beautiful gardens add a nice touch. Don't expect modern conveniences. Ask for a room with a balcony. Across the street is the Renaixença, owned by the same proprietors. Both hotels open only in summer. Ph.: 93-894-83-75. Call for rates.

If you're willing to stay outside of town (about 7 miles), La Masia Casanova is a true men's retreat with a clothing-optional pool, sauna, Turkish bath, and Jacuzzi. Rates: $120–$160; Ph.: 93-818-80-58; www.masiacasanova.com.

BARCELONA

Barcelona is thirty minutes by train from Sitges, so you have your choice: stay in Barcelona and sojourn to Sitges or stay in Sitges and reverse commute. It all depends on whether you want a city vacation or a beach vacation. Either way, spend at least a few minutes in one of the world's most elegant cities. (And of course you'll want to check out the Gaudí architecture, if you can stomach it).

Hotel Axel (33 Calle Aribau; www.axelhotels.com/en/; 93-323-93-93). A gay hotel that is "hetero-friendly." Rooftop pool and bar, in-house gym, several bars. The social meeting place for upscale gay tourists in Barcelona.

Cal Pepe (Plaça de les Olles) is a tiny seafood restaurant with giant flair. It's a little out of the way, which makes it popular with locals and ex-pats. Forget about trying to decide what to order—you sit at the bar and take what the chef gives you.

Bars in Spain get busier later than in the U.S. And since more people go to bars, you can expect to see heavy traffic on the streets at 4 a.m. as people head home. Zeltas (75 Calle Casanova) is a good bet. So is Sweet, which is right next door and has less attitude. Clubs in Barcelona, as in any city, are always changing. But check out Metro Disco (185 Calle Sepulveda) and Salvation (19–21 Ronda Sant Pere).

The downside of staying in Barcelona is that return trains from sitges stop running very early. If you stay out late, you may end up having to find a room in Sitges anyway (if you can).

FOR THE ART LOVER

Check out the two El Grecos at the Museu Cau-Ferrat in Sitges. Admission is 4 Euros. Free first Wednesday of the month; closed Mondays. Ph.: 93-894-03-64; www.mnac.es.

Bedding (Not So Gay)

Hotel Calipolis (2 Av. Sofia). Right on the sea. Built in the sixties, the Calipolis has a modernist feel with nice views of the ocean. Ph.: 93-894-15-00; www.hotelcalipolis.com; check the Web site for rates.

The gleaming white Terramar (80 Passeig Maritim) was the first grand hotel in Sitges and has become a local landmark. It has over 200 rooms, a restaurant, tennis courts, and access to a golf course. Ph.: 93-894-00-50; www.hotelterramar.com; call for rates.

DAY TRIP

If you're in the mood for a little old-world charm, take a day trip to Vilafranca del Penedès, a town with a long winemaking tradition. There's a history of winemaking museum that offers tastes, too.

QUOTE

"I don't know whether you've ever looked into a miner's eyes—for any length of time, that is. Because it is the loveliest blue you've ever seen. I think perhaps that's why I live in Ibiza, because the blue of the Mediterranean, you see, reminds me of the blue of the eyes of those Doncaster miners."

—Bisexual writer Alan Bennett, "The Pith and Its Pitfalls" (1981)

In and Out

Train service from Barcelona costs about $3. You can catch the train to Sitges at the RENFE/metro stations Plaça de Sants or Passeig de Gràcia.

Ibiza

We were standing outside at 4 a.m., after hours of drinking and dancing at a cavelike club, waiting for a local (a friend of a friend of a friend) to find a moped he could borrow to get us to his car so that he could show us the other side of the island (because he insisted that we couldn't leave without seeing it). Such is life on Ibiza.

Ibiza is one of the Balearic Islands. It is located in the Mediterranean, just south of Spain. The downside of Ibiza is its drug-drenched, megaclub, 24-hour drunken party scene—both straight and gay. In July and August drunken Australian tourists (and tourists from the rest of the world) abound. Privilege, one of Ibiza's famed nightspots, is said to be the largest dance club in the world. This is not a resort destination for adults. Fortunately, things calm down by the end of the summer (the island is practically deserted by mid-September), and it's possible to get a taste of the island's actual beauty while still enjoying its laissez-faire ambience.

The Old Town of Ibiza City, known as Dalt Vila, is ruled over by a fourteenth-century cathedral with a drawbridge that invites visitors into town. Here you'll find plenty of restaurants, pizza joints, and shops selling Ibiza-themed trinkets. If you arrive by cruise, this is where you will dock. Fortunately, it's also the capital of the city's gay scene.

Ibiza has several cities, some rowdier and more drunken than others. The beer-drinking heterosexual Brits tend to congregate in Sant Antoni de Portmany, so it's best to stay far, far away.

Sand

Ibiza's gay beach is Playa Es Cavallet, not far from Playa Salinas. The half-mile beach has a wild, natural feel, which makes it popular with straight nudists. The crashing waves attract a fair number of windsurfers. It's located about five miles from Ibiza town. While at the beach, you can quench your thirst or have a seaside lunch at Chiringay (17 Playa Es Cavallet), where you can also rent your umbrella or pick up a bottle of sunscreen. If you need a break from the gay scene, head to Playa Salinas. It's straight but satisfyingly chic.

Calories

Los Pasajeros (6 Carrer Vicente Soler, Old City) has good, cheap food. Ca'n den Parra (3 Carrer San Rafael, Old City) offers terrace dining with nice views of the

A BRIEF HISTORY
OF THE SPEEDO

(otherwise known as the "competition brief," "swim brief," "posing brief," "racing brief," "budgie smuggler," and the "banana hammock")

The Speedo swimwear company has been around since the 1920s, but it wasn't until the 1950s that the classic men's "racer brief" as we know it came into use. At the 1956 Olympics in Melbourne, the much-beloved (or, depending on your sexual orientation, much-reviled) Speedo made its official debut.

With clothes getting tighter and tighter in the seventies (have you seen an episode of *The Six Million Dollar Man* lately? When Steve Austin goes jogging in his white jogging suit, it looks almost obscene,) men around

old city. Studio (4 Carrer de La Virgen 4, Old City) is very popular with the gays. Try to get a table on the terrace overlooking the Plaça de Sa Drassaneta.

Macao Café (11 Plaza de Sa Riba, Old City) is slightly more upscale. Good for a romantic dinner for two.

Bar Tab

Ibiza's nightlife changes all the time, but the island's famous megaclubs include:

the world started wearing tight-fitting bikinis. I have vivid memories of my father, post-divorce, hitting on flight attendants and other bathing beauties by his L.A. pool in his skimpy Speedo and gold chain necklace.

In Europe, Speedos were actually mandated at many pools as a way to keep men from wearing their street shorts in the water, whereas in America they always carried a tint of degeneracy (some beach communities actually banned them).

In the 1980s, the increasing visibility of gay men in American culture led to a new brand of homoanxiety among straight men. Real men, it was decided, didn't wear Speedos. This anti-Speedo brand of homophobia has spread via Hollywood movies and American television to foreign lands, and one sees fewer and fewer Speedos on the beaches of Europe anymore—except, of course, where gay men congregate.

Privilege. Allegedly the largest club in the world. Bring a suit for the swimming pool. www.privilege.es.

Amnesia. Home of the so-called "Balearic Beat." The club runs a bus from the Old Town every twenty minutes 11 p.m.–3 a.m. www.amnesia.es.

Heaven. In walking distance from Old Town. Part of a European chain of clubs.

Space. Parties go twenty-four hours (and longer). www.space-ibiza.es.

Bedding

Aparthotel Navila (1 San Luis, Old Town). Located on a quiet street in the heart of old town. A surprisingly good deal. Ph.: 971-39-05-73. Call for rates.

Hotel Montesol (2 Paseo Vara de Rey). In the center of Old Town, the Montesol has been popular since it opened in the 1930s. Be prepared for loud noise at night from the streets below. Simple rooms without great charm. Ph.: 971-31-01-61. The website is in Spanish: www .hotelmontesol.com.

Hotel Marigna. Situated on Windmill Hill in Figueretas, this exclusively gay hotel is about a fifteen- to twenty-minute walk from Old Town. With forty-four rooms, the Marigna bills itself as Europe's largest all-gay hotel. There's a nearby bus stop to the gay beach. $50–$150 (expect a seven-night minimum stay in August); Ph.: 971-30-49-12; Web: www.hotelmarigna.com.

Hotel Hacienda Na Xamena is a luxury resort far from the island's party scene. Not by any means a gay hotel, expect five-star service and prices. The hotel offers a forty-five-minute "wellness journey" through several seawater pools, each offering a unique and spectacular view. Ph.: 971-33-45-00; www .hotelhacienda-ibiza.com. Contact the hotel for rates.

In and Out

The airlines offer cheap tickets from almost all the European cities to Ibiza, so it may make more sense to do a little genuine sightseeing first rather than flying directly to Ibiza from the States. The British equivalent of Orbitz is www.easyjet.com.

You can reserve an airport shuttle to your hotel at www.resorthoppa.com or catch a taxi, which, at slightly less than the shuttle, will cost you about $15 into town. There is also a bus (the #10) that runs every thirty minutes.

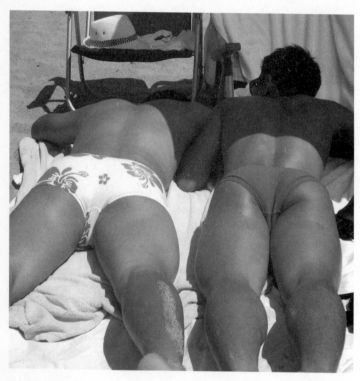

Boys in bikinis.

CHAPTER TEN

Puerto Vallarta, Mexico

PUERTO VALLARTA may conjure up images of Julie and the Love Boat, but these days an RSVP cruise with a thousand-plus guys would be more apt. Puerto Vallarta has become the gay capital of Central America, a major stop on the GLBTQ Grand Tour. Because it's so much cheaper south of the border, a Vallarta vacation can be highly cost effective, even if you're coming from the East Coast. (Last I checked, round-trip from New York was only $595 with fourteen days' advance notice).

Vallarta is on Mexico's West Coast, making it a popular destination with cruises embarking from L.A. and San Diego. Because it's on the Pacific, the sunsets are spectacular. The water may not be as vivid blue as in Cancún, but the crowds are more refined. Even the residents themselves are middle-class (with a 96% literacy rate) and there are many American ex-pats who have settled in town. Vallarta appeared on the tourist map as a result of the Hollywood film *Night of the Iguana,* starring Richard Burton. Unlike some other Mexican tourist destinations, Vallarta is an actual city, with a historic old town, not just a collection of high-rises built

Q FACT

Puerto Vallarta is in the state of Jalisco, essentially the capital of Mexico's tequila industry, though tequila isn't actually produced in Vallarta itself.

up to cater to foreigners. But because it has become a major tourist destination, almost everyone speaks English.

Vallarta's climate is tropical, which means you can visit any time of the year, but summer tends to be humid and vaguely oppressive. During the summer, you can practically simmer in the sea, but that does make for excellent diving conditions.

When booking your hotel, you are definitely going to want to stay in the area known as the Romantic Zone. It's not just the gay area, it's also the most popular part of Puerto Vallarta. The Romantic Zone is in Old Vallarta, which also includes El Centro. El Centro has charming cobblestone streets and whitewashed houses, but because it is built on the hillside, expect a serious hike anywhere you go.

Hotels in Mexico are rated by the government, which means the rating system is highly formulaic. A high rating means many amenities, but not necessarily any elegance or style. A gorgeous boutique hotel can lose out simply because it doesn't have room service.

MONTEZUMA'S REVENGE

Once upon a time, bottled water was a fanciful notion that only made sense when visiting third-world countries. Now we're so used to paying for water, we do it without giving it much thought. While in New York City, you're actually better off drinking water straight from the tap, in Mexico, buying bottled water remains a very good idea.

Sand

The gay beach is known as Blue Chairs, so nicknamed for the blue lounge chairs (thankfully shaded by thatched umbrellas) that spread out in front of a restaurant named, guess what, Blue Chairs. Head to the south end of Los Muertos Beach, the most popular beach in Vallarta. The beach is just a quarter-mile south of the pier at Francisca Rodríguez Street. In case you can't see the blue chairs in the glare of the Mexican sun, the restaurant flies a rainbow flag. If you're taking a taxi to the beach, you can tell the driver "Blue Chairs, Los Muertos,"

Q FACT

Street numbers in Puerto Vallarta do not follow a logical order. Like it or not, you will have to rely on the instincts and knowledge of your cab driver to get around.

and he'll know exactly where to go. Don't be afraid to venture into the area increasingly known as Green Chairs—it too is gay friendly. If you want to bring your own towel, this is a public beach, so don't feel obliged to rent a chair.

Nude sunbathing is at a remote beach reachable only by boat: Paco's Hidden Paradise, 12 miles south of Puerto Vallarta. Boats depart from Los Muertos pier (not far from Blue Chairs). The journey takes two hours through beautiful Banderas Bay (you may very well see dolphins

BUDGETING YOUR KNICKNACKS

If you've ever been to Mexico or the Caribbean, you will be used to the barrage of trinket-sellers who descend on tourists like flies on dung. Expect to be hawked everything from jewelry to fruit to blankets. Most people feel the need to prove themselves by bargaining down the sellers. What could be worse, after all, than being laughed at by a Mexican seller who got an extra two bucks for an overpriced necklace? Hmmm, maybe spending one's vacation worrying about being laughed at by said Mexican salesperson? I recommend deciding over breakfast how much you plan to gamble on knickknacks over the course of the day and then gambling away the preset amount—not more or less. It will take virtually all the stress out of your vacation.

dancing in the water), and the booze-cruise boat ride is part of the experience. For 650 pesos ($70 U.S.), you will get a Hans Christian 41 sailing yacht, three hours on the island, all food aboard, open bar on the boat and on the island, and snorkeling gear. (Premium bar and

OTHER GAY DAY-TRIP OPTIONS

One option for the more serious nature enthusiast is Oscar Frey's Ocean Friendly Tours. Frey, an oceanographer studying humpback whales, operates gay whale-watching tours on Banderas Bay (whether the whales are gay or not is another question). With Frey's specialized equipment, you'll actually get to listen to the whales singing underwater. Whale season is December 15 to March 31. www.oceanfriendly.com.

Diana DeCoste hosts several lesbian cruises on Thursdays. www.dianastours.com.

You could also try horseback riding. Boana's Tours begin at a ranch north of Vallarta, from which you ride up the hillside through the tropical forest to the river, where you can swim. A restaurant at the top of the hill means you don't have to pack a lunch. Transportation to/from the ranch is included. www.boana.net/tours .htm.

PVRPV offers gay cruises similar to Rainbow Dancer's on Fridays from 10 a.m.–3 p.m., with boarding at 9:30 a.m. www.pvrpv.com.

wines available for an extra charge). You'll have key lime pie onboard as you return to Puerto Vallarta. The cruise operates on Wednesdays and Fridays (and is not to be confused with their Saturday afternoon cruise, which does not stop at a beach.) Web: www.rainbow dancer.com.

Bar Tab

Most of the gay bars are right in the Romantic Zone. Things don't get going till one or two in the morning. Until then, head for Olas Altas Street, which is lined with sidewalk cafés.

Antropology (101 Morelos, Plaza Rio, El Centro). A stripper bar free-for-all.

Apaches (439 Olas Altas, Olas Altas). Small and elegant with sidewalk seating.

Blue Sunset Rooftop Bar. The Blue Chairs Resort's rooftop bar, good for watching the sun set.

Encuentros (312 Lázaro Cárdenas). Tres chic.

Flicker Sky Lounge (228 Ignacio Vallarta Street). Watch a classic movie under the stars at this mixed rooftop lounge.

Garbo (142 Pulpito). Often has live entertainment.

Hotel Mercurio (168 Francisca Rodríguez, Zona Romantica). This hotel bar is open to everyone, but it's the gays who dominate.

Mañana (290 V. Carranza, Romantic Zone). Vallarta's big club. Well air-conditioned. Open every night until 6 a.m.

Club Paco Paco (278 Ignacio L. Vallarta). Once the biggest party in town.

Paradise VIP (240 Lázaro Cárdenas). A lesbian bar.

THE ZIP LINE

I love the Zip Line—you know, the thing where you go speeding through the air over a valley harnessed only to a thin rope strung between two trees. Why am I such a fan? Because saying "I did the zip line" makes you sound extremely cool and brave. But unlike most other outdoor activities, doing a zip line requires no skill whatsoever. It's impossible to get it wrong. They strap you in the harness and you go. You may have to deal with your fear of heights, but other than that, you can't fail. There's nothing to push, nothing to pull and you don't have to worry about having good balance.

I don't know of any all-gay zip-line excursions, but that only makes the whole experience that much more of a machismo booster. Check out El Eden and Canopy Tour Los Veranos, two companies specializing in zip-line adventures.

Plasma Video Bar (235 Piño Suarez). Features a back-room maze.

The Ranch (239 Venustiano Carranza). A stripper bar with a cowboy theme.

Vallarta Cora Hotel Courtyard (174 Pilitas). The most popular all-men's pool party in Vallarta.

Calories

Lunch is the big meal of the day in Mexico. Find a good restaurant, sit down, eat your heart out, and then hit the beach for an afternoon siesta. Many restaurants offer "international cuisine," which usually means steaks, pastas, and a few Mexican specialties.

Brazil (210 Venustiano Carranza). Perfect for anyone on a high-protein, low-carb diet. All the meat you can eat. Choose from a vast array of shish kebabs—delivered to your table continually until you can't eat any more.

Chez Elena (520 Matamoros). Eat where Richard Burton wooed Elizabeth Taylor and where Peter O'Toole, Anthony Quinn, and Robert Shaw escaped the glare of the Hollywood media. Have the Sate Mixto, their signature dish: an Indonesian brochette of pork, beef, and shrimp in an exotic peanut and spice sauce.

El Arrayan (344 Allende). A new arrival on the Vallarta scene with country-style Mexican food. Located in El Centro.

Gaby's (252 Mina). Family-run, authentic Mexican.

Red Cabbage (204A Rivera del Rio). Gourmet Mexican.

Roberto's Puerto Nuevo (284 Basilio Badillo). Great seafood and generous portions.

Q HINT

Choco Banana (147 Amapas).
ChocoBanana is a standby of gay Vallarta, beloved for their phallically shaped, eponymous desserts.

Trio (264 Calle Guerrero). Superb food makes this a favorite.

Bedding (Gay)

Vallarta's specifically gay hotels tend to be simple affairs, compared to the grandiose retreats that cater to families.

Blue Chairs (Los Muertos Beach). For those who want to be at the epicenter of Vallarta's gay world. Don't expect much luxury or personalized service, but you can fall out of your room onto the beach. Rates: $69–$229; Ph.: 866-514-7969; www.bluechairs.com.

Vallarta Cora (174 Pilitas). Better known for its sexually charged scene than for its charm. All rooms have a view of the action by the pool. Basically a cross between a hotel and a sex club. Ph.: 322-222-6234; www.vallartacora.com; call for rates.

Villas David (348 Calle Galeana). Classic gay guesthouse with clothing-optional areas. Located in El Centro. Rates $93–$119; Ph.: 322-223-0315; www.brads.net/davidpv.

Mercurio (168 Francisca Rodríguez). Not the prettiest hotel, but very centrally located. The rooms do not have phones or air conditioning. Rates: $84–$100; Ph.: 322-222-4793; www.hotel-mercurio.com.

Bedding (Not So Gay)

Hacienda San Angel (336 Calle Miramar). You will not only be close to the gay area, but you will fall in love—at least with your hotel. Not only are the furnishings at this boutique establishment sumptuous and tasteful, the proprietors have thought of little things that make guests very, very happy—like free calls to the U.S. Only in Mexico—where hotels sometimes take up many acres—could a property with three swimming pools be called "boutique," but that distinguishes it from its all-inclusive neighbors. Rates: $235–$620; Ph.: 877-815-6594; www.haciendasanangel.com.

Tropicana (214 Calle Amapas). Right near the gay beach. Low on comfort (read, no air conditioning—make sure your room at least has a fan), but great prices and good location. Part of an international chain. Rates: $69–$84; Ph.: 322-222-0912; www.hoteltropicana.com.

If you are so inclined, Vallarta has many all-inclusive resorts, but none of them are particularly close to the gay area.

In and Out

Continental, Delta, and American all fly direct, non-stop to Puerto Vallarta from New York (the flight takes 8 hours). Puerto Vallarta's airport is Aeropuerto Internacional Gustavo Díaz Ordaz, about five miles north of downtown. The best way to get to your hotel is via taxi. But even so, you will have to purchase a taxi voucher just outside the arrivals area. The vouchers are priced by zone. (If you happen to get suckered into taking a time-share van instead of a taxi, you will be subjected to a hard sell for the length of your ride.)

CHAPTER ELEVEN

Rovinj: Croatia's Gayest Resort

PERFECTLY CLEAR WATER, plenty of nude men from throughout Europe, and freshly grilled meats make for happy summer days on the beaches of Rovinj, a picturesque town on the coast of Croatia. An up-and-coming resort, Rovinj is still overwhelmingly straight, but the gay beach is increasingly popular with Europeans searching for something new. If you want to visit a gay beach in a beautiful European setting that most Americans will never have heard of, head to Rovinj, or, as it is known in Italian, "Rovigno."

Rovinj is located on the northern coastline of Croatia, directly across the Adriatic from Venice, and has long been influenced by Italian food and culture. Some say it is more Italian than Croatian. The closest major Croatian city is Zagreb, about 100 miles away. Rovinj is built on a hill, at the top of which sits the beautiful Cathedral of St. Euphemia, built in 1736.

Don't be surprised if you never run into another gay person while you're in town (my friends and I didn't, anyway). Rovinj gets many visitors, few of them gay. But the gay beach gets so crowded each day that it can be hard to find a spot. Speaking of hard, the "beaches" are composed of giant rock plateaus, not sand.

Croatia has only recently become familiar to Americans, but it has long been a tourist destination for Europeans, who appreciate its extensive coastline and over a thousand coastal islands. Rovinj dates from before Roman days, and was eventually part of the Venetian empire. Rovinj has also been ruled by the French, the Austrians, the Fascists, and the Germans. In the second half of the twentieth century Rovinj was, like all of Croatia, a part of Yugoslavia, which disintegrated in 1991.

Croatia's official policies on homosexuality are very liberal (the age of consent for all sexual activity is 14, regardless of gender, and same-sex partnerships are legally recognized). But as a Central European country and former socialist republic, there is a good deal of homophobia and most gays and lesbians are still in the closet. Interestingly, Croatia has exceptionally liberal attitudes toward heterosexual behavior. Croatia's beaches are known for attracting nudists from around the world. In Rovinj, the beach next to the gay beach is actually a swingers', beach, and it is not uncommon to see couples having sex *en plein air.*

Sand

The gay nude beach is known as Cape Cross or Punta Kriza. (For many years it was Monsena beach, but that beach was bought by a private company hostile to gays.) To get to Punta Kriza, drive to the Amarin resort (yes, in Rovinj you will need a rental car). Behind the parking lot there is a small dirt road. From there, it is about one mile to the end of the road. Park wherever you can, and start walking. You will pass the straight nude beach and eventually arrive at the gay section. Wear comfortable shoes and don't carry more than you need to, because the walk can be precarious at places. Be sure to pack a pair of water shoes (or buy some in town at one of the many local stands); you will need them on the sharp, rocky seabed.

Calories

Rovinj is a coastal town, so you'd be wise to enjoy plenty of fish and seafood. Matteo's Grill in the Old Town is a great choice.

At most of the beaches you will find improvised restaurants. The gay/naturist beach has its own grill with excellent roasted meats and fish, as well as tasty potatoes. The gays tend to sit in one section, the straights in another.

Ice cream is extremely popular in Rovinj: you will see people eating it for breakfast. You can get a cone or a more elaborate sundae at numerous places on the main square.

For a more traditional breakfast, head to the Hotel Adriatic on the main square. There are dozens of café tables out front.

Bar Tab

Rovinj is not known for its nightlife. It has one gay bar, outside of town, that doesn't even have a name. In town, on the main square, impressively decorated Zanzibar is the place to go if you want to feel extremely hip. The Café Bar Batel (27 Zdenac) is a nice option if you want a more intimate ambiance and coffee with a splash of liqueur.

LOVE, SEVENTIES STYLE ON THE COAST OF CROATIA

Croatia has a well-deserved reputation as the capital of European nudism. Beaches along the coastline and the islands (and there are thousands of them) cater to nudist sunbathers. But we're not talking old-fashioned "let's-play-volleyball-in-our-sneakers-and-socks" nudism. Croatian nudism—at least on the quaint, island resort of Rovinj—is a full-blown, 1970s-style outdoor orgy.

I only know this because you have to walk by the straight beach to get to the gay one. Each journey to and fro, we were treated to a quarter-mile spectacle of heterosexual coupling (mostly fellatio and cunnilingus, but we saw a little of everything). The great irony was that when you got to the gay beach, the boys were far more prim and proper in their Speedos and swimming trunks. When the gay guys wanted to get it on, they went into the woods on the hill for some discretion.

Let's face it: from a voyeuristic perspective, the straight beach was far more fun. Alas, there didn't seem to be much mingling between the straights and the gays. In fact, there was at least one straight guy intent on expressing his homophobia at the local café. But for the most part, everyone just minded their own business. Well, their own business and the business of all the others at the public sex show.

Bedding

There are no gay hotels in Rovinj, but there are several nice establishments. You may also want to consider renting an apartment.

Villa Angelo D'Oro (Vladimira Švalbe 38–42). An upscale boutique hotel in the center of town. All twenty-four guest rooms are furnished with antiques and feature air conditioning and satellite TV. Ask for a room with a view of the sea. Rates: $60–$300; Ph.: 385-52-840-502; www.rovinj.at.

Hotel Adriatic (P Budicin bb). The oldest hotel in Rovinj, with lots of charm. Located right on the main square. Ph.: Contact Hotels.com at 800-804-6835. Call for rates. For private accommodations, visit www.croatia-gay.com, e-mail croatia@croatia-gay.com, or call 36-30-685-2643. You can also try www.adriatica.net or www.dalmatia.net, two Internet room-booking services.

In and Out

Rovinj is served by two airports, Pula Airport and Vrsar Airport. You'll need to fly through Zagreb.

You can also take a high-speed ferry from Venice for approximately $75 round-trip. For details, visit www.aferry.to (prices are in British pounds). Note: There's no ferry service to or from Rovinj on Monday or Tuesday, so take that into consideration when booking your trip through Venice. Also, make careful note of the ferry terminal name (Stazione Marittima San Basilio) as Venice has numerous ferry terminals. Also, be aware that Rovinj has two ports (one by the town square, and one on the opposite side of town) and your ferry may arrive and depart from different ports.

A gay beach is the perfect escape.

Gay Beach Travel Tips

The Gay Pack

Perhaps because we do not typically travel in the traditional family unit, but still crave a sense of connectedness, gays often seem to cluster in "travel packs." A group of friends and/or friends of friends will rent a house together, or share a couple of hotel rooms, and suddenly a new form of family is born.

Like any family, a gay pack can be just as much about tension and low-grade resentment as warmth and conviviality. A few tips when traveling *ensemble:*

1. If possible, meet as a group ahead of time. Go for a drink or dinner. Get to know each other a little before suddenly going on vacation. Sharing a house for a week can strain even the closest friendships.
2. Give up gossip. Gossip is fun for a moment, hell for eternity. A single negative comment about one of your fellow travelers will inevitably come back to haunt you. It doesn't matter what your friend's boyfriend does in the dunes or at the dinner table, keep all conversation light and friendly.

3. Discuss expectations (especially about expenses). Nothing breeds resentment faster than disagreement over who owes what. Make sure you have paid your fair share.

Eating Out

Don't order the cheeseburger in a seafood place and don't order the tilapia in a burger joint. When in Rome, eat pasta. When in Tokyo, eat rice.

Decide what you want before you call over the waiter or waitress. If you waste their time at the beginning of your meal, expect to have your own time wasted for the remainder of the evening.

The "special" may be the freshest item in the house or the thing that needs to be pushed before it goes bad. Ask your server for the inside scoop.

Seafood Studies 101

No, this is not a lesbian sex guide. It's a vocab primer for ordering dinner in coastal towns. Since the best beach resort restaurants tend to lean more toward the surf than the turf, it's important to know your dolphin from your tuna. Always ask your server what's fresh.

Moules: mussels. The French love mussels and there's actually a restaurant in Paris that only serves buckets of these black-shelled critters (and fries on the side). They say you're not supposed to eat the ones that are hard to open.

Bass: a firm white fish.

Bouillabaisse: A French fish soup. If it is served properly, spread some of the garlic paste on your croutons and turn them upside down onto the soup.

Catfish: I'm Jewish and we don't eat things with whiskers or anything that looks like whiskers. But if you're feeling Southern, go for it.

Calamari: A few years ago, no one had heard of calamari. Now you can't avoid them. Squid rings, for the uninitiated.

Ceviche: Raw seafood salad with a little lemon. I'll pass, thanks.

Cioppino: The Italian version of bouillabaisse.

Clams: Tougher than oysters. Better deep-fried than raw.

Clams casino: Clams baked with chopped bacon and herbs.

Clam chowder (New England or Boston style): The white kind, made with cream.

Clam chowder (New York style): The red kind, made with a tomato base.

Cod: A dense white fish that has a mild flavor, is low in fat, and flakes easily. The classic prep-school meal.

Flounder: Better than its name suggests.

Haddock: Basically the same as cod and sometimes called scrod.

Halibut: A heavier fish that's more substantial than most.

Herring: The national food of Sweden. The Swedes love their herring, especially pickled. The English prefer their herring smoked or "kippered."

Mahi Mahi: Also known as dolphin, but completely unrelated to Flipper. A thick, white fish similar to swordfish.

Oysters: A more sophisticated taste than clams. Eat raw with a little lemon. Avoid fried oysters: they're too soft to be battered.

Snapper: Maybe the tastiest fish of all. Order it grilled with a wedge of lemon.

Tilapia: Similar to red snapper or orange roughy.

Great Gay Beach Reads

The last ten years have seen a constant stream of GLL—gay lite lit—flowing into bookstores. While you can't tell a book by its cover, it's often fun to read a book just because you know the cover will get you some attention. Below are some great beach reads for your summer vacation:

William Storandt, *The Summer They Came*. A group of forward-thinking gays turns a sleepy resort into a hot gay destination.

Armistead Maupin, *Tales of the City*. The classic that inspired the miniseries.

Alex Sanchez, *Getting It*. A teen novel that will delight gays of any age.

Ben Tyler, *Tricks of the Trade*. The lightest of lite lit, but that's what makes it fun. If nothing else, buy it for the cover.

Michael Thomas Ford, *Last Summer*. Ford has a delightful ability to weave together the stories of a cast of gay characters.

Joe Keenan, *My Lucky Star*. Keenan is brilliant, and this novel is his best.

Dave Benbow, *Summer Cruising*. A murder mystery set on an Atlantic cruise. Come on, what more do you need when you're sunning on the beach?

Bed-and-Breakfast Dos and Don'ts

If you have seen *Flirting With Disaster* (and if you haven't, rent it immediately), then you'll know that some people just aren't "B&B" people. Are you? Before checking into a B&B, it's good idea to discuss this important identity issue with your therapist (and partner). Below are some basic rules to follow when staying at, or considering staying at, a B&B.

When booking your reservation, be sure to ask if the bathroom is private or shared. If it's shared, how far away will it be from your room?

B&Bs tend to have limited reception times. Be sure to arrive close to when you said you would, or at least call in advance to let the owners know of any change in plans.

Don't let the dogs or cats out the front door unless informed that this is acceptable.

Keep noise to a minimum.

At breakfast, have the blueberry pancakes. Make polite conversation with your fellow breakfast companions. (Unless it is a specifically gay inn, polite conversation does not include any discussion of religion, politics, or sex toys.)

At the end of your vacation, tip the housekeeping staff a few dollars for each night's stay.

Sign the guestbook with a smile. (This is not the place for critical feedback for the inn owners!)

What to Pack

On some trips, I've gone for weeks with nothing but what I could stuff into a knapsack. Other times, I've brought a full wardrobe for one night, so I know there's

no "right" way to pack. But I think the following for-
mula works well for a three- to five-day vacation:

2 Speedos
1 boxer-cut swimsuit (you never know when you might
    feel shy)
Running shorts
Dress shorts
1 pair of jeans
1 pair of long pants
2 polo-style short-sleeved shirts
3 T-shirts (at least one white for daytime and one black
    for nighttime)
A light jacket
A cotton sweater
Flip-flops
Sneakers (for dancing)
Underwear
Suntan lotion
Aloe (it works like magic if you get burned)
Aspirin
Toiletries
Motion sickness pills (if you plan on doing any boating
    excursions)
Books
Sunglasses
Compact umbrella

Gay Beach Etiquette

1. If you bring a boom box, don't sit down near anyone who's sleeping or reading.

2. Bring enough beer or soda to make a few friends.
3. *Never* laugh, giggle, or scoff at other sunbathers whom you do not know. If you must comment on a fellow beachgoer's dress, manner, or appearance, wait till you're back in the hot tub.
4. If you're playing volleyball or Frisbee, invite others who look interested to join you. At all times, be polite and welcoming.
5. Don't leave any trash behind. Take all your items with you.

Traveling Solo

Many guys are intimidated by the thought of traveling by themselves, and I admit it can be daunting. But there are numerous advantages—not the least of which is being able to dictate your own schedule. A few simple tricks will help you make friends quickly.

1. Make eye contact. It's amazing to me how many guys don't. Eye contact invites conversation. Of course, if your boyfriend is back home, that's another story, but then, why are you traveling to a gay beach alone?
2. Leave your iPod in the hotel room. A guy with plugs in his ears looks unapproachable.
3. Leave your watch in the hotel room, too. "Do you know the time?" is a great conversation starter.
4. Ask someone to apply sunscreen to your back. I know it's bold, but skin cancer is unacceptable and what's a better way to get to know someone quickly than by rolling over and letting him have his way with you?

5. Carry a book but don't bury yourself in it. A book allows others to start conversations with you. "Is that good? I've seen it in the store." You might want to think about a friendly response ahead of time.

6. Don't judge your vacation by whether or not you get laid. This is a mistake many gay men make, but it only leads to disappointment. (If it doesn't on this trip, it will on the next one.) Figure out another way to measure your satisfaction: by the number of books you read, the number of great conversations you have, or the number of friends you make.

7. Be the first to strike up conversation. People are afraid of looking foolish and getting rejected. If you say "hello" first, you will ease their fears.

Further Reading

John Preston, ed. *Hometowns: Gay Men Write About Where They Belong* (NY: Plume, 1992) is a collection of essays by well-known gay writers. Included are essays on Provincetown, Fire Island, and Key West.

Once upon a time, Fodor's issued gay travel guides written by gay travel expert Andrew Collins. The books are out of print, but remain informative and useful. See *Fodor's Gay Guide to the USA* (2001), *Fodor's Gay Guide to New York City* (1997), *Fodor's Gay Guide to San Francisco and the Bay Area* (1997), *Fodor's Gay Guide to South Florida* (1997), and *Fodor's Gay Guide to Los Angeles and Southern California* (1997).

Also unfortunately out of print (but available used through Amazon) is *Frommer's Gay and Lesbian Eu-*

rope (2003) by David Andrusia, Memphis Barbree, Haas Mroue, and Donald Olson.

Some other out-of-print guides include Out & About Gay Travel Guides' *USA Cities* (1997) and *USA Resorts and Warm Weather Vacations* (1997).

Useful Web Sites

www.gay.com
www.outtraveler.com
www.gaymart.com/travel/world.html

Acknowledgements

Too many people deserve thanks for me to name them individually, but a special acknowledgement must be made to Admir Imami, David Galbraith, Jimmy Markee, Kevin O'Connor, Paul Langland, and Mykel for their support with this book. Thank you, mom, for telling me to write it.